BEST FESTIVALS

MID·ATLANTIC

BEST FESTIVALS

MID·ATLANTIC

Over 250 Festivals from New York State to Virginia

DALE ADAMS

The Countryman Press
Woodstock, Vermont

No entries for any of the festivals listed in this book have been solicited or paid for.

Library of Congress Cataloging-in-Publication Data
Adams, Dale, 1956-
    Best festivals mid-Atlantic: over 250 festivals from New York to
Virginia/Dale Adams
        p. cm.
    Includes indexes.
    ISBN 0-88150-222-7
    1. Festivals—Middle Atlantic States. 2. Middle Atlantic States—
Social life and customs.   I. Title.
GT4805.5.A34   1992
394.2'6'0974—dc20   91-42455
                                    CIP

10 9 8 7 6 5 4 3

Published by The Countryman Press, Inc.
Woodstock, Vermont 05091
Printed in the United States of America
Printed on recycled paper
Cover and text design by Virginia Scott

Photo Credits
Cover photograph and photograph on page 93 by Jim Russell/Harbor
Festivals, Inc.; page 7 by Adirondack Daily Enterprise; page 56 by Ron
Keinhaus/Clearwater; page 81 by Deborah Bornstein Gichan; page 101 by
Ron Romanski/Reading Eagle Co.; page 126 by Goschenhoppen Historians,
Inc.; page 131 by Hub Willson/Musikfest; page 138 by Augusta Heritage
Center; page 170 by Judy Kramer/Fairfax County Council of the Arts; page
191 by Cornelius Hogenbirk/Chatsworth Cranberry Festival; page 203 by
Chris Spencer/West Virginia Pumpkin Festival; all other photographs by
the author.

Acknowledgements

I owe many thanks to my contacts in the state tourism offices: Mara Barlow of the New Jersey Division of Travel and Tourism, Arlene Booth of the New York Division of Tourism, Lynn Neuman of the Pennsylvania Bureau of Travel Marketing, Colleen O'Toole of the Maryland Office of Tourism Development, Lisa Seagroves of the West Virginia Division of Tourism and Parks, Judy Watkins of the Virginia Division of Tourism, and Gigi Windley of the Delaware Division of Tourism Marketing. These individuals helped me obtain information from local tourism offices, reviewed my draft list of festivals for their state, and provided information, comments, and encouragement through the whole process.

—D. A.

Contents

Introduction

In Brooklyn at the Feast of Our Lady of Mt. Carmel, 130 men lift a three-ton, six-story tower holding an Italian orchestra. Carrying it down the neighborhood streets, sometimes they dance the cha-cha, sometimes they drop to the ground and quickly lift the structure, and sometimes they spin it completely around.

At the Virginia Highland Games in Alexandria, husky men in kilts throw 130-pound, 20-foot poles end over end, competing for the straightest, longest throw. Other men throw long-handled hammers, iron weights, and bags of straw.

In the mountains of north-central Pennsylvania, when the village of Noxen holds its Rattlesnake Roundup, people go into the forest, catch snakes, and bring them back to a pen at the festival grounds. At the end of the hunt, prizes are awarded for the longest rattlesnake, the longest combined length of two snakes, and the snake with the most rattles.

If you want to see something different, go to a festival.

In the spring, at the Feast of the Ramson, the people of Richwood, West Virginia, forage in the woods for ramps—wild leeks known for their persistent odor—and then cook them up and serve them with ham, bacon, fried potatoes, beans, corn bread, and hot sassafras tea.

When shad return to the Delaware River to spawn in the spring, Lambertville, New Jersey, holds its Shad Festival. On the banks of the river, local groups serve the fish charcoal-broiled and as gumbo, cakes, chowder, and dumplings.

In Pennsylvania, the McClure Bean Soup Festival, first held more than a hundred years ago as a reunion for Civil War veterans, still serves Union Army bean soup of navy beans, hamburger, and lard, cooked in big iron kettles over wood fires.

1

If you want to taste something different, go to a festival.

At the Kutztown Folk Festival in Pennsylvania, a man in a floppy hat and oversized tie stands on a stage in a large open-air pavilion and tells Pennsylvania Dutch jokes (some of them racy) in the local Dutch dialect.

At First Night, the New Year's Eve celebration in Annapolis, Maryland, a black woman in traditional African dress tells lively stories and folktales to an engrossed crowd of both young and old.

At St. Anthony's Italian Festival in Wilmington, Delaware, a 50-member accordion orchestra accompanies a large, balding opera tenor singing "O Solo Mio."

At the Vandalia Gathering in Charleston, West Virginia, an elderly woman from deep in the backwoods of the state sits before her audience with an old banjo, playing the "old timey" songs of the Appalachian Mountains.

If you want to hear something different, go to a festival.

For new experiences, festivals are hard to beat; and festivals of the mid-Atlantic states are especially fun because of the region's diversity. With communities that range from mountain villages in West Virginia to Jewish neighborhoods in Manhattan, the mid-Atlantic offers a multitude of opportunities to experience another culture, another way of life.

At festival time, communities open their doors. The people come outside to enjoy food, music, dance, crafts, and competitions. For the most part, these activities are not contrived; they represent each community's local culture and traditions. These people are celebrating life in their corner of the world. And, best of all, they are inviting us to celebrate with them.

Using This Guide

This book contains more than 260 of the best festivals of the mid-Atlantic region: New York, New Jersey, Pennsylvania, Delaware, Maryland, the District of Columbia, Virginia, and West Virginia. Nearly all kinds of festivals are represented here, including arts festivals, ethnic festivals, food festivals, music festivals, and folklife festivals. Not included are festivals that are actually music, theater, or film series.

The festivals are organized by month and then broken down by state in the rough order of their calendar date. Every month is represented, but most festivals occur from May through October. Each festival entry provides the general date of the festival, such as "first weekend in May." The entries also give admission fees; however, it is best to call for current information, since fees are prone to change.

A telephone number for festival information is also given. *Always call to confirm dates, times, and other important information.* It is not unusual for a festival to change its date or location, and sometimes changes are made nearly at the last minute. Another telephone number is included for tourist information (if it is different from the festival information number). This is useful for locating accommodations near the festival. Many of the rural and small-town festivals offer an opportunity to combine the trip with a stay at a country inn or bed and breakfast.

This book was compiled with the help of state tourist officials, local tourist promotion agencies, and a number of other resources. Festival entries are based on information provided by the festival organizers. Although an exhaustive search was made to find the best festivals, no doubt some are missing. Readers are invited to suggest festivals for the next edition or to point out inaccuracies in the descriptions of those included here. Please write: Festival Editor, The Countryman Press, P.O. Box 175, Woodstock, VT 05091.

Have a good time!

January

New York

A Festival of Lights

Niagara Falls, N.Y., Saturday following Thanksgiving until early January.

See November—New York.

Snowtown U.S.A.

Watertown, N.Y., last full weekend in January to first weekend in February.

Watertown is known for its harsh winters and snow; nine feet of snow fell during one recent December. In the midst of the snow season, the city celebrates with 10 days of activities. At the New York State Snow Sculpting Competition, artists compete for the state title and a chance at the national title, which is held in Wisconsin. Other competitions include snow softball, snowmobile races, fishing derbies, hockey tournaments, and dogsled races. One downtown circle is flooded to form a huge ice skating rink; another is the site of a wintertime block party. Entertainment includes a country music jamboree, dinner theater, and concerts.

Admission: free; charges for some events.
Location: various locations throughout the city and county.
Information: 1000 Islands International Council, (800) 847-5263 or (800) 547-5263 (in New York).

Winterfest

Syracuse, N.Y., last weekend in January to first weekend in February.

A snow castle and giant snow sculptures of cartoon characters are built in downtown Syracuse during Winterfest. The 10-day festival celebrates midwinter in New York's snow country, and the "weatherproof" schedule of events offers both outdoor and indoor activities. One Saturday there's an outdoor chowder cook-off, the next a hot chili cook-off. Chefs of the Northeast compete in the ice-carving competition; runners brave the cold in the Frostbite Run; and three-person and four-person teams compete in "smooshing," racing together on one pair of snow skis. Winterfest also offers Friday-night band concerts and dances, senior citizen card-game tournaments, cartoon film festivals on the two Saturdays, and horse-drawn wagon rides. Winterfest attracts more than 200,000 people; most activities are scheduled for the weekends.

Admission: free; charge for some events.
Location: downtown and various locations in Onondaga County.
Information: Syracuse/Onondaga Convention and Visitors Bureau, (800) 234-4797 or (315) 470-1800.

February

New York

Snowtown U.S.A.

Watertown, N.Y., last full weekend in January to first weekend in February.

See January—New York.

Winterfest

Syracuse, N.Y., last weekend in January to first weekend in February.

See January—New York.

Saranac Lake Winter Carnival

Saranac Lake, N.Y., first full week in February.

Considered America's oldest winter festival, the Saranac Lake Winter Carnival was started almost 100 years ago as a diversion for tuberculosis patients. Ever since the first carnival, an Ice Palace has been built with blocks of ice from Lake Flower. Blocks measure about four feet by two feet by the thickness of the ice (which can be as much as three feet), and weigh from 400 to 750 pounds. Modern machinery and nineteenth-century ice-industry tools are used to cut, remove, and position the blocks. Over 1,500 blocks are used to create an elaborate palace 80 feet or longer in length, with turrets rising to 40 feet. After the fire department coats the finished structure with a light spray, it is adorned with colorful lights.

The Saranac Lake Winter Carnival runs for a week from the first Saturday in February to the following Sunday. Festivities of the week include the Coronation of the Winter Carnival Royalty, broom-hockey games, a figure-skating show, a Kiddie Parade, a ski-slope inner-tube race, and the Rotary Club Variety Show. The second weekend offers the most activities, including pancake breakfasts, a cross-country ski race, winter volleyball, Paul Smith's College's old-time lumberjack demonstration, a Gala Parade through the village, a Carnival Ball at Hotel Saranac, a teen dance, snowshoe softball, and a Sunday-night fireworks display over the Ice Palace.

Admission: free.
Location: throughout the village.
Information: Saranac Lake Chamber of Commerce, (800) 347-1992 or (518) 891-1990.

Ice Palace at the Saranac Lake Winter Carnival.

Cooperstown Winter Carnival

Cooperstown, N.Y., weekend in middle of February.

In the middle of the frigid upstate New York winters, the people of Cooperstown shake off cabin fever with a winter carnival. Held Friday through Sunday, the event features outdoor events like an ice sculpture contest, horse-drawn-wagon rides, a Chilly Willie Scavenger Hunt, sled races, and volleyball on ice. Indoor activities generally include a bowling tournament, a children's talent show, evening dances, and athletic competitions. Through the weekend, churches and community groups sponsor pancake breakfasts, soup luncheons, and warming tents with hot food and drinks.

Admission: free.

Location: throughout village.

Information: Cooperstown Lions Club, P.O. Box 912, Cooperstown, NY 13326.

Tourist Information: Cooperstown Chamber of Commerce, (607) 547-9983.

March

Maryland

Maryland Days Weekend

St. Mary's City, Md., weekend nearest Maryland Day, March 25.

On March 25, 1634, the first settlers in Maryland celebrated a Mass of Thanksgiving at St. Clement's Island. They built a capital city at St. Mary's City on land they had purchased from the Yeocomico Indians. However, St. Mary's City was the capital only until 1694, when it was abandoned. Today the site is a museum with archaeological excavations, reconstructed structures, and an authentic working re-creation of a 1630s square-rigged ship, the *Maryland Dove*.

Maryland Days is celebrated at the historic site in the afternoon of the Saturday and Sunday closest to the holiday. The program features a seventeenth-century militia encampment, rigging and seamanship demonstrations on the *Maryland Dove*, and musical performances by southern Maryland entertainers. Music has included sea chanteys, gospel, bluegrass, and progressive rock. Local community groups serve Chesapeake Bay seafood, southern Maryland stuffed ham, pork barbecue, and ethnic foods that represent the state's diversity.

Admission: free.

Location: Governor's Field of Historic St. Mary's City.

Information: Visitor Services, Historic St. Mary's City, (301) 862-0990.

Tourist Information: St. Mary's Chamber of Commerce, (301) 884-5555.

New York

Central New York Maple Festival

Marathon, N.Y., weekend in late March or early April.

Most of Marathon's 1,050 inhabitants help with the Maple Festival, which attracts about 100,000 people. They tap the village's maples, boil down the sap at the sugar shack, cook up pancake breakfasts, participate in the Maple Festival Queen pageant, park cars, organize entertainment, and perform hundreds of other tasks. There is a juried art show and continuous entertainment at the Marathon High School. The village's churches hold bake sales, quilt shows, and chicken barbecue dinners. The Maple Museum sells maple syrup, maple lollipops, maple-sugar candy, and maple sundaes. At Lovell Field, the volunteers offer pony rides, give helicopter rides, and run tours of the sugar shack. Many festivalgoers avoid traffic and make the trip more fun by riding the New York, Susquehanna, and Western Railway from Cortland to Marathon. The festival runs morning and afternoon on Saturday and Sunday.

Admission: free.
Location: throughout village.
Information: Central New York Maple Festival, (607) 849-3278.
Tourist Information: Cortland County Chamber of Commerce, (607) 756-2814.

Pennsylvania

Beaver County Maple Syrup Festival

Fallston, Pa., last weekend in March or first weekend in April.

At the Beaver County Maple Syrup Festival, 10,000 people enjoy all-you-can-eat pancake and sausage meals served with maple syrup produced at Brady's Run Park. The two-day feast requires 200 gallons of syrup, 3,000 pounds of pancake mix, 2,200 bushels of buckwheat groats to grind, 800 bushels of wheat, 600 bushels of corn, and 2,500 pounds of sausage. Visitors to the festival can also tour the sugar bush (the stand of maples being tapped) and the sugar shack (the building where the syrup is made), watch a tomahawk- and knife-throwing competition, see native American dancing, or witness a Civil War reenactment. Musical entertainment includes country-and-western singers, bluegrass bands, and Highlander pipe bands. The festival runs morning and afternoon on Saturday and Sunday.

Admission: free.

Location: Brady's Run County Park.

Information: Beaver County Conservation District, (412) 774-7090.

Tourist Information: Beaver County Tourist Promotion Agency, (800) 564-5009 (in area code 412) or (800) 342-8192 or (412) 728-0212.

Pennsylvania Maple Festival

Meyersdale, Pa., week in late March or early April.

In the winter of 1948 a group of men gathered around the potbellied stove in the Shipley Hardware Company Store in Meyersdale and began planning the community's first maple festival. Today, 50,000 people come to the festival throughout the week for all-you-can-eat pancake and sausage dinners, country entertainment, a quilt show, a classic car show, the Grand Feature Parade, and coronation of the Maple Queen. Many of the activities are held at Festival Park, which has a restored eighteenth-century home and re-created doctor's office, country store, and cobbler shop. Entertainment has included historical pageants, an Eastern European dance troupe, bluegrass music, and cloggers.

Admission: adults, $3; senior citizens, $2; ages 12–18, $1; under 12, free with parents.

Location: Festival Park and uptown area.

Information: Pennsylvania Maple Festival, (814) 634-0213.
Tourist Information: Laurel Highlands, Inc., (800) 333-5661 or
(412) 238-5661.

Virginia

Highland Maple Festival

Monterey, Va., second and third weekends in March.

The southernmost maple syrup festival is held in Highland County,
"Virginia's Switzerland." Held over two weekends, it offers tours
of the county's sugar camps, arts and crafts at several locations,
and entertainment that includes clogging, storytelling, bluegrass
and country music, and juggling. The Wooly Ram Round Up, the
Maple Sugar Hoedown, and the Buckwheat Stomp are some of
the dances held Friday and Saturday nights. Community groups
offer pancake or buckwheat cake breakfasts, served with local
syrup and country sausage, ham, or bacon. Allegheny Mountain
trout dinners, featuring locally raised trout, are also served.

Admission: free.
Location: Monterey and Highland County.
Directions: Monterey is located at the junction of U.S. routes 220
and 250. From Staunton, Virginia, take 250 west for 45 miles.
Information: Highland County Chamber of Commerce, (703)
468-2550.
Tourist Information: Alleghany Highlands Chamber of Commerce, (703) 962-2179.

April

Delaware

Hagley's Irish Workers' Festival
Wilmington, Del., last Saturday in April.

Hagley is the original du Pont mills, estate, and gardens, now a museum open to the public. The 230 acres along the Brandywine River include the 1803 du Pont home, the restored workers' community, a restored machine shop, and the du Pont's nineteenth-century French Garden. Hagley celebrates the contributions of Irish workers, who once labored in the du Pont mills, with a one-day festival in April. The festival features Irish entertainment, including Irish step dancers performing four-hand jigs and three-hand reels. Past performers have included Trikkiwikkit, a Celtic musical trio; balladeers Liam Maguire and Tony Kelliher; and Fair Isle, which performs traditional and contemporary folk music of Ireland, Scotland, and England. Irish food, like ham and cabbage, is served.

Admission: adults, $9.75; senior citizens and students, $7.50; children ages 6–14, $3.50; children under 6, free.
Location: Hagley Museum.
Information: Hagley Museum, (302) 658-2400.
Tourist Information: Greater Wilmington Convention and Visitors Bureau, (800) 422-1181 or (302) 652-4088.

Colonial marchers in the National Cherry Blossom Festival parade.

District of Columbia

National Cherry Blossom Festival

Washington, D.C., week beginning Sunday before April 7.

The National Cherry Blossom Festival begins with the lighting of the huge, 300-year-old ceremonial Japanese lantern at the Tidal Basin. The stone lantern is over eight feet high and weighs 6,000 pounds. The famous cherry trees that surround the Tidal Basin were a gift of friendship from the people of Japan in 1912. In 1965 the Japanese gave another 3,800 trees, which were planted around the monuments. The thousands of cherry trees around the Tidal Basin and along the Mall blossom in late March or early April, attracting thousands of tourists.

Now more than 50 years old, the National Cherry Blossom Festival is scheduled during blossoming time. The week includes a fashion show, free concerts in downtown parks, the Cherry Blossom Ball and crowning of the Cherry Blossom Queen, and a marathon race. The highlight of the week is the Cherry Blossom

Festival Parade on Saturday, with lavish floats, giant helium balloons, and some of the country's finest marching bands.

Admission: free; charges for various events.
Location: various locations in Washington.
Information: National Cherry Blossom Festival, Inc., (202) 737-2599.
Tourist Information: Washington, D.C., Convention and Visitors Association, (202) 789-7000.

New Jersey

Shad Festival

Lambertville, N.J., last full weekend in April.

Each spring the shad swim up from the Atlantic to spawn in the Delaware River. Sitting on the east side of the river, Lambertville celebrates the annual migration with a Shad Festival. Through the weekend, a row of booths sells shad gumbo, shad cakes, shad chowder, shad dumplings, smoked shad, and shad ravioli. On Sunday afternoon, a shad dinner on the banks of the Delaware offers hearty portions of chowder, charcoal-broiled shad, baked potato, coleslaw, rolls, and tea or coffee.

New Jersey's only commercial shad fisherman lives in Lambertville and gives demonstrations in the seine technique of shad fishing, which the Indians taught the colonial settlers. The stage on North Union Street offers musical entertainment, including folk, rock, blues, and bluegrass. Other activities include a juried arts and crafts show, historical tours, children's storytelling, and the Shad Hop at the Elks Club Saturday night.

Admission: free.
Location: downtown Lambertville.
Information: Lambertville Area Chamber of Commerce, (609) 397-0055.

New York

Central New York Maple Festival

Marathon, N.Y., weekend in late March or early April.

See March—New York.

Stuyvesant Park Festival

New York, N.Y., Sunday in mid-April.

Stuyvesant Park was once the early nineteenth-century farm of the Stuyvesant family, and trees the family planted still grow on the four-acre urban park. Manhattan's first major spring festival is held there in April as a fund-raiser for the local neighborhood association. Vendors line Second Avenue, selling crafts, antiques, collectibles, and a variety of international foods. Held on a Sunday afternoon, the festival also offers on-stage entertainment. Past acts have included a honky-tonk piano player, magicians, and folk singers.

Admission: free.
Location: Second Avenue from 14th to 23rd streets.
Information: Great Events, (212) 689-4543.
Tourist Information: New York Convention and Visitors Bureau, (212) 397-8222.

Pennsylvania

Beaver County Maple Syrup Festival

Fallston, Pa., last weekend in March or first weekend in April.

See March—Pennsylvania.

Pennsylvania Maple Festival

Meyersdale, Pa., week in late March or early April.

See March—Pennsylvania.

Virginia

International Azalea Festival

Norfolk, Va., mid-April.

When thousands of azalea bushes bloom in Norfolk's Botanical Garden, the city salutes the North Atlantic Treaty Organization (NATO), whose North American headquarters is located in Norfolk. Each year one NATO nation is honored, and a young woman from that country reigns as Queen Azalea. Princesses, each representing the remaining NATO countries, make up her court. The ambassador from the honored country is invited to crown the queen during the Saturday-afternoon coronation at the Botanical Gardens.

The International Azalea Festival runs Wednesday through Sunday. A Grand Parade, with international floats, marching bands, and military units from across the country, is held in Norfolk Saturday morning. Highlights of the festival are the air shows at the Norfolk Naval Air Station, which feature precision-flying teams, vintage airplanes, parachute jumps, and wing-walking demonstrations. There are also performances by the U.S. Navy Blue Angels and the U.S. Navy Leap Frogs. Another highlight is the number of events featuring the art, music, and food of the honored NATO nation.

Admission: most events free.

Location: various locations in Norfolk.

Information: Hampton Roads Chamber of Commerce, (804) 622-2312.

Tourist Information: Norfolk Convention and Visitors Bureau, (804) 441-5266.

British and Irish Festival
Norfolk, Va., fourth weekend in April.

Colorful bagpipers, eighteenth-century artisans, re-created medieval battles, English morris dances, and British and Irish music
are among the many activities scheduled at Norfolk's British and
Irish Festival. Eight stages provide continuous entertainment,
including such groups as the Firefighters Emerald Society Pipe
Band, the Blackthorn Stick Ceili Dancers, the Khedive Highlanders, the Scottish Country Dancers, and Spectrum Puppet Theatre.
In areas of the festival grounds representing each country are
sheepdog demonstrations, brass rubbings, the Guinness Gold Cup
Dart Tournament, and artisans and crafters. Vendors sell currant
cakes, meat pies, bangers, Irish soda bread, fish and chips, British
roast beef, bridies, and ales and beers. The festival runs Friday
evening, Saturday afternoon and evening, and Sunday afternoon.

Admission: free.
Location: Town Point Park.
Information: Festevents, Ltd., (804) 627-7809.
Tourist Information: Norfolk Convention and Visitors Bureau,
(804) 441-5266.

West Virginia

Feast of the Ramson
Richwood, W.Va., second Saturday in April.

Each spring, people of the Appalachian Mountains go into the
woods to collect ramps, or wild leeks. Many West Virginia communities put on ramp feasts, with ramps fried up and served with
ham, beans, and corn bread. The breath and perspiration of those
who eat ramps is said to reek for days—and these people like it.
In the days before refrigeration, ramps were eaten as a spring
tonic: the plant is one of the first greens to appear.

The NRA in Richwood, West Virginia, doesn't protect the rights of gun owners. Here, NRA stands for the National Ramp Association, and Richwood is the ramp capital of the world. The editor of the local newspaper promoted that fact one time by mixing a concoction that smelled like ramps in his ink; the post office admonished him for his odoriferous newspapers. On a Saturday in April the NRA, in cooperation with the Sisterhood of Sippin Sizzlin' Sassafras, puts on the Feast of the Ramson, with fried ramps, ham, bacon, fried potatoes, brown or white beans, corn bread, and hot sassafras tea. Cloggers, gospel singers, and country-and-western bands entertain throughout the day; the festival also features arts and crafts, a 10-kilometer Ramp Run, and white-water kayak races.

Admission: free, charge for dinner.
Location: Richwood High School.
Information: Richwood Area Chamber of Commerce, (304) 846-6790 or (304) 846-6433.

May

Delaware

Delmarva Hot-Air Balloon Festival
Milton, Del., Memorial Day weekend.

As a benefit for the American Diabetes Association, the First State Balloon Team holds a Memorial Day weekend balloon festival in rural southern Delaware. The festival not only includes balloon launches mornings and evenings, but entertainment, tethered balloon rides, a flea market, a crafts show, and children's games and rides during the day. On-stage entertainment scheduled for the afternoon has included performances by the Commodores, the U.S. Navy's jazz band, and by the First State Force, a band composed of Delaware police officers.

Admission: free.
Location: Milton Medical Associates grounds, 424 Mulberry Street.
Information: Delmarva Hot Air Balloon Festival, (302) 684-2000.
Tourist Information: Chamber of Commerce of Milton, (302) 684-1101.

Maryland

Maryland Sheep and Wool Festival
West Friendship, first full weekend in May.

A highlight of the Maryland Sheep and Wool Festival is the

Sheep-to-Shawl Contest, where each team competes to shear a sheep and make a shawl from its fleece. Each team, consisting of one shearer, three spinners, and one weaver, is judged both on time and quality of the job. For instance, the shearer is judged on control of the sheep and its appearance after shearing. The shawl must be of a certain size. After the competition, each shawl is displayed and auctioned off, with the proceeds going to the team.

The Maryland Sheep and Wool Festival is considered to be the largest event of its kind in the country. Other competitions include 4-H and F.F.A. sheep judging, live lamb and carcass judging, a sheep-shearing contest, and the Maryland Grand Lamb Cook-Off. At the Sheep Breeds Display Barn, about 30 different breeds are exhibited. The festival also offers sheep dog demonstrations, sheep farming and wool production seminars, and a fleece show and sale. Over 200 craft and supply booths sell wool garments, sheepskins, spinning wheels, rugs, and other wool items. The festival also offers country entertainment and food, including many lamb dishes.

Admission: free.
Location: Howard County Fairgrounds, Route 144 and Fairgrounds Road.
Information: Howard County Tourism Council, (410) 750-8582.

Towsontown Spring Festival

Towson, Md., first weekend in May.

Towson, a suburb of Baltimore, welcomes spring with a weekend street festival. Held since 1968 and attracting about 300,000 people, the event offers continuous entertainment on four stages both afternoons. The Wine Garden features an oldies show, and past performers have included Gary U.S. Bonds and the Grassroots. The Beer Garden offers Baltimore-area rock groups, the Information Booth Stage offers street performers, and the Children's Entertainment Stage offers jugglers, nature programs, singing, and parachute games. Twelve streets in Towson are closed and filled with nearly 400 booths selling crafts and food. The festival also includes a judged art and photography show, an antique car show, and a flea market.

Admission: free.
Location: Towson Court House grounds and surrounding streets.
Information: Towsontown Spring Festival, (410) 825-1144.
Tourist Information: Baltimore County Office of Promotion and Tourism, (410) 887-8040.

Bay Bridge Walk and Bayfest
Annapolis, Md., first Sunday in May.

Nearly 20 years ago, a Boy Scout leader from Baltimore noticed that one of the two spans of the Bay Bridge had been closed for repairs. Thinking that a walk across the bridge, high above the Chesapeake Bay, would be a neat adventure for his troop, he asked the transportation department to let them on the span one Sunday. His request was denied, but the idea caught the attention of Maryland's Secretary of Transportation, Harry Hughes, who initiated a yearly "holiday" when a span of the Bay Bridge would be closed for pedestrians to enjoy.

Now, more than 50,000 people walk the four miles across the bridge, enjoying a warm spring Sunday with spectacular views of the Chesapeake Bay. From about 9 a.m. to 4 p.m., buses transport the walkers from parking lots in Annapolis to the east end of the bridge. After reaching the west end at Sandy Point State Park, bridge walkers can enjoy Bayfest, with music, exhibits, and Chesapeake Bay seafood. Profits from the festival benefit the Chesapeake Bay Trust, a nonprofit organization that promotes bay educational programs and restoration projects.

Admission: free.
Location: Chesapeake Bay Bridge and Sandy Point State Park.
Directions: park at the Navy-Marine Corps Stadium, Anne Arundel Community College, or Kent Island Shopping Center and take the free shuttle bus to the bridge.
Information: Chesapeake Bay Trust, 60 West Street, Annapolis, MD 21401.

Tourist Information: Annapolis and Anne Arundel County
Tourism Office, (410) 280-0445.

Maryland Preakness Celebration

*Baltimore and other places in Maryland, nine days before
the Preakness Stakes (third Saturday in May).*

The Preakness Stakes, the second jewel of horse racing's Triple
Crown, runs the third Saturday in May at Baltimore's Pimlico
Race Course. The preceding nine days are filled with more than
a hundred events, beginning with a huge parade in downtown
Baltimore. Other events include a hot-air balloon race, a great
schooner race on the Inner Harbor, and the Triple Crown Ball.
There are concerts, block parties, and horse shows at various
locations through the state. There is also a number of children's
activities, such as the Pee-Wee Preakness, where children race
hobbyhorses. One of the final events is the infield party the day
of the race, with infield concerts, competitions, and food.

Admission: $2 Preakness Pin for most events.
Information: Maryland Preakness Celebration, (410) 837-3030.
Tourist Information: Baltimore Area Convention and Visitors
  Association, (410) 659-7300.

National Pike Festival

*Washington, Allegany, and Garrett counties, Md., third
weekend in May.*

Now U.S. Route 40, the National Pike was the first national road
crossing the Appalachians to the western frontier. The original
section, from Baltimore to Cumberland, Maryland, resulted from
Thomas Jefferson's proposal for a national road in 1806 and was
financed by the banks. A later section from Cumberland to Wheeling, West Virginia, was the first road to receive federal funding.
  On the third weekend in May, communities along a 200-mile

stretch of the road through western Maryland and southwestern Pennsylvania celebrate the road with a festival they have called the "longest festival in the world." Lions clubs put on chicken barbecues, Boy Scouts demonstrate Indian dances, country bands perform in parking lots, churches make turkey dinners, clubs hold antique car shows, and museums hold special programs. During the weekend, wagon trains travel the road, with scheduled stops in each community, and there are muzzle-loader demonstrations and buckskinner camps.

Admission: free.
Location: towns and villages along U.S. Route 40.
Information: Allegany County Tourism, (301) 777-5905; Washington County Tourism, (800) 228-7829; Deep Creek Lake-Garrett County Promotion Agency, (301) 334-1948.
Also see May—Pennsylvania.

Chestertown Tea Party Festival

Chestertown, Md., last Saturday in May.

In 1774, a few months after the Boston Tea Party, the British closed the port of Boston to all trade until restitution for the destroyed tea had been made. When this news reached Chestertown, Maryland, the angered citizens held a public meeting. The *Geddes*, a trade ship carrying a small amount of tea, had dropped anchor off Chestertown, and the citizens quickly made it unlawful to bring in the tea, sell it, consume it, or in any way assist in its distribution. However, the tea in the hold of the *Geddes* still angered local residents, and on May 23, 1774, a mob boarded the *Geddes* and threw the tea into the Chester River.

Chestertown now celebrates its own tea party with a one-day festival, which begins in the morning with a colonial parade featuring the Tench Tilghman Fife and Drum Corps and the Maryland First Regiment. The highlight of the day is the tea party reenactment, when a crowd of angry citizens gathers at Town Park and then marches to the river, where it boards a ship and throws boxes of tea overboard. Through the day there are tall ships, craftspeople, colonial music and dancing, storytelling, and

Eastern Shore delicacies like crab cakes, chitterlings, and fried chicken.

Admission: free.

Location: High Street.

Information: Chestertown Tea Party Festival, Inc., (410) 778-1630.

Tourist Information: Kent County Chamber of Commerce, Inc., (410) 778-0416.

Hometown Holidays

Rockville, Md., Memorial Day weekend.

Rockville's biggest event of the year fills the Memorial Day weekend with continuous music, an arts and crafts show, laser light and fireworks shows, an antique show, and the Memorial Day parade. Stage entertainment and roving musicians perform each afternoon. Headliner performers are scheduled for Saturday and Sunday evenings, with rock musicians like Martha Reeves, Junior Walker and the All Stars, and Blood, Sweat and Tears on Saturday night, and classical groups like the National Chamber Orchestra on Sunday.

Admission: free.

Location: Middle Lane parking Lot.

Information: City of Rockville Recreation and Parks, (301) 309-3330.

Tourist Information: Conference and Visitors Center of Montgomery County, (301) 428-9702.

New York

Lilac Festival

Rochester, N.Y., begins second Friday in May and runs 10 days.

Rochester's Highland Park holds 1,200 lilac bushes, covering 22 acres and representing more than 500 species. In mid-May when the lilacs bloom, the city celebrates with a 10-day festival. The kick-off event is the Saturday parade through Rochester. Each afternoon singers, bands, and dancers perform on two outdoor stages in the park, and in the evenings national entertainers and local groups appear at the downtown festival tent. The events of the week include a bonsai exhibition, road races, art shows, and special entertainment for children, such as singers, jugglers, stiltwalkers, clowns, and puppet shows.

Admission: free; charges for some activities.
Location: Highland Park and downtown Rochester.
Information: Greater Rochester Visitors Association, Inc., (716) 546-3070.

Tulip Festival

Albany, N.Y., Mother's Day weekend.

Albany's Tulip Festival was first held in 1949, but it has its roots in the Dutch Pinksters Festival held in Albany in the seventeenth century. The event begins Friday at noon with the mayor's official proclamation, followed by the scrubbing of State Street by Dutch maidens in wooden shoes. On Saturday and Sunday, Washington Park, with 50,000 blooming tulips, is the setting for Pinksterfest, which offers more than 250 food and crafts vendors and afternoon entertainment. Performers have included gospel choirs, folk singers, blues singers, opera groups, and country-and-western bands. Kinderkermis, a children's program, offers jugglers, clowns, magicians, and storytellers. The weekend also includes the Tulip Queen Coronation, a bicycle race, and a Saturday night Tulip Ball.

Admission: free; charges for some events.
Location: Washington Park.
Information: Mayor's Office of Special Events, (518) 434-2032.
Tourist Information: Albany County Convention and Visitors Bureau, (800) 258-3582 or (518) 434-1217.

Ukrainian Festival
New York, N.Y., third weekend in May.

Pierogi (dumplings stuffed with potatoes, meat, sauerkraut, or cheese), holuptsi (stuffed cabbage), borscht (beet soup), and kobasa sausage are some of the Ukrainian specialties served at the Ukrainian Festival. Held in the streets near St. George's Ukrainian Catholic Church in Manhattan's Little Ukraine, the festival also offers craft demonstrations such as embroidery, *pysanky* (Easter eggs), and woodcraft. On-stage performances usually include Ukrainian dancers, bandura (a three-stringed instrument similar to the lute) groups, and Ukrainian ensembles. Dumka, a Ukrainian choir, sings inside St. George's Church, which is built in the Ukrainian Byzantine style with mosaic art, stained glass windows, and a dome. The festival runs through the afternoon and evening Friday, Saturday, and Sunday.

Admission: free.
Location: Seventh Street, between Second and Third avenues.
Information: St. George's Ukrainian Catholic Church, (212) 674-1615.
Tourist Information: New York Convention and Visitors Bureau, (212) 397-8222.

Ninth Avenue International Food Festival
New York, N.Y., third weekend in May.

It's a mile-long gastronomic extravaganza—vendors selling the food of more than 32 countries line a 20-block stretch of Ninth Avenue. Black beans and rice, kabobs, tempura, ravioli, Swedish crepes, roast lamb, tacos, kielbasa, corn dogs, moussaka, gazpacho, zeppole—it's all there. The good food can be enjoyed with music and dance on three stages. Past performers have included country-and-western bands, reggae groups, Middle Eastern dancers, woodwind quintets, American folk dancers, and barbershop quartets. The festival runs through the afternoon and evening both Saturday and Sunday.

Admission: free.
Location: Ninth Avenue from 37th to 57th streets.
Information: Ninth Avenue Association, (212) 581-7029.
Tourist Information: New York Convention and Visitors Bureau, (212) 397-8222.

Fabulous Fifth Avenue Street Fair

Brooklyn, N.Y., Sunday one week before Memorial Day.

Celebrating the revitalization of Park Slope, the Fabulous Fifth Avenue Street Fair features a parade, marching bands, hundreds of street vendors, and two stages of Brooklyn's most promising performers. The ethnic diversity of the Park Slope neighborhood gives the fair the atmosphere of an old-world bazaar, with foods from around the world, crafts, rides, antiques, art, and clothing. Entertainment scheduled also reflects this diversity, with Latin jazz and salsa, Caribbean music, gospel, soul, Andean and American folk, rock and roll, and Polish polka music. The festival generally runs through the afternoon on Sunday.

Admission: free.
Location: Fifth Avenue in Park Slope, from Flatbush Avenue to 18th Street.
Information: Park Slope Fifth Avenue, (718) 965-2826.
Tourist Information: New York Convention and Visitors Bureau, (212) 397-8222.

General Clinton Canoe Regatta

Bainbridge, N.Y., Memorial Day Weekend.

The world-championship flat-water canoe race follows the Susquehanna River for 70 miles from Cooperstown to Bainbridge. This endurance race attracts the best professionals from North America; recent winners have come from Michigan and Quebec. The flat-water canoe race occurs on Memorial Day, capping off a weekend of races, that also include sprint, cruising, and recreation competitions.

The races all end at the General Clinton Park, which offers wrestling tournaments, carnival rides, arts and crafts, and balloon launches. Entertainment has included a marching-band field show and stage performances by local musicians. The Kids' Korner features ventriloquists, jugglers, magicians, and performing poodles.

Admission: $2.
Location: General Clinton Park.
Information: General Clinton Canoe Regatta, (607) 967-8700.
Tourist Information: Leatherstocking Country, New York, (800) 233-8778 or (315) 866-1500.

Pennsylvania

Pittsburgh Children's Festival

Pittsburgh, Pa., second week in May.

Both children and adults enjoy the many activities of the Pittsburgh Children's Festival. Decorated with colorful banners and pennants, the festival grounds are filled with large tents, food booths, and performance stages. Strolling performers in outrageous costumes entertain a crowd at one location, while not far away a Dixieland band marches by, followed by a handful of children dancing behind it. Young children are delighted when a larger-than-life teddy bear stops to chat; others explore their creative talents at the face-painting booth. Entertainment is only half of it: children can take a paddleboat ride, learn how to juggle, participate in a crafts workshop, join a physical skill competition, or visit the petting zoo.

The main attraction of the Pittsburgh Children's Festival is the series of performances scheduled through the morning and afternoon all five days. Besides American entertainers, the acts include professional companies from all over the world. Past festivals have featured Soviet acrobats, Japanese drummers, Scot-

tish puppeteers, Finnish dancers, Afro-American storytellers, and
Norwegian clowns. The shows are held in theaters in the West
Park neighborhood during the festival, which runs from Wednes-
day through Sunday.

Admission: West Park activities, $1, free with show ticket; each
show, $4.50 at gate, $3.50 in advance; family sampler tickets
available.
Location: West Park.
Information: Pittsburgh Children's Festival, Inc., (412) 321-5520.
Tourist Information: Pittsburgh Convention and Visitors
Bureau, (800) 366-0093 or (412) 281-7711.

Mercer Museum Folk Fest

Doylestown, Pa., second full weekend in May.

The tall, concrete Mercer Museum looks like a castle with its
various wings and assortment of windows. Henry Mercer, an
archaeologist and anthropologist, designed this unusual building
in the first decade of the twentieth century to house his collection
of early American tools. Inside, a lofty well reaches from the
ground floor to the roof. On surrounding balconies, farm implements, Colonial furniture, cider presses, and other relics are
displayed. Heavy agricultural implements, Conestoga wagons,
and other cumbersome objects extend into the well, suspended by
wires and chains.

At the Mercer Museum Folk Fest, a hundred skilled artisans
demonstrate the eighteenth- and nineteenth-century crafts that
are represented in the museum's exhibits. Special demonstrations have included timber framing, baking in a squirrel-tail oven,
boiling soap, stringing a rope bed, and flax-breaking to make
linen. Folk music and dancing, jugglers, and a medicine show
have provided entertainment, and the Northamptontowne Militia
has depicted military life between 1774 and 1782. Brunswick
stew cooked over an open fire, a colonial dinner, and a picnic-
basket-lunch auction are some of the meals usually served.

Admission: adults, $6; senior citizens, $4; children ages 9–17, $4;
children 8 and under, free; family with own children, $15.

Location: grounds of the Mercer Museum, 84 South Pine Street.
Information: Bucks County Historical Society, (215) 345-0210.
Tourist Information: Bucks County Tourist Commission, Inc.,
   (215) 345-4552.

National Pike Festival

*Somerset, Fayette, and Washington counties, Pa., third
weekend in May.*

The National Pike Festival commemorates America's first transportation link from the east to the western frontier. Thomas
Jefferson proposed the National Pike in 1806, and soon the first
section, from Baltimore to Cumberland, was built with bank
funding. Later the federal government financed lengthening the
road to West Virginia. Through its history many prominent figures have traveled the National Pike, including then-lieutenant
colonel George Washington, P. T. Barnum, and Charles Dickens.
   On the third weekend in May communities along the National
Pike—now U.S. Route 40—in Maryland and Pennsylvania participate in "the longest festival in the world." Wagon trains travel
along the highway, fire companies put on chicken barbecues,
museums hold special programs, country-and-western bands perform, craftspeople demonstrate period work, and church groups
hold flea markets.

Admission: free.
Location: towns and villages along U.S. Route 40.
Information: Washington County Tourism, (412) 222-8130;
   Laurel Highlands, Inc., (800) 333-5661 or (412) 238-5661.
Also see May—Maryland.

Mayfair

*Allentown, Pa., Thursday through Monday of Memorial
Day weekend.*

Allentown's community celebration offers over 200 free performances in four different park settings. Music is featured, and past festivals have included performances by doo-wop singers, polka bands, the Sammy Kaye Orchestra, Maynard Ferguson, classic rock groups, country music singers, and country fiddlers. Dancers, storytellers, comedians, puppeteers, and acting groups also perform.

Mayfair runs all day on Thursday and Friday and through the afternoon and evening on Saturday, Sunday, and Monday. The festival also offers juried art, photography, and sculpture exhibitions. A juried artists' market offers high-quality crafts and artwork for sale. In addition to a variety of activities for children, there are fun events like a pet-and-owner look-alike contest and a boomerang demonstration.

Admission: free.

Locations: Cedar Beach Park, the Rose Garden, West Park, Union Terrace Park, Muhlenberg College, and Cedar Crest College.

Information: Mayfair, Inc., (215) 437-6900.

Tourist Information: Lehigh Valley Convention and Visitors Bureau, (800) 747-0561 or (215) 266-0560.

Mifflinburg Buggy Days

Mifflinburg, Pa., Memorial Day Weekend.

A century ago, Mifflinburg was known as "Buggy Town." After the Civil War, quality craftsmen turned the community into a renowned buggy- and sleigh-making center, with as many as 20 shops producing 6,000 vehicles a year. Not surprisingly, the industry collapsed within a few years of the advent of the automobile. The William A. Heiss Coach Works was abandoned and left undisturbed until a decade ago when it became the town's Buggy Museum. Mifflinburg celebrates Buggy Days on the Saturday and Sunday before Memorial Day with buggy rides, arts and crafts, traditional foods like shoofly pie and raisin pie, down-home music, and demonstrations of buggy making at the museum.

Admission: free.

*Buggy rides at Mifflinburg
Buggy Days.*

Location: streets surrounding Mifflinburg Buggy Museum.
Information: Mifflinburg Buggy Museum, (717) 966-1666.
Tourist Information: Susquehanna Valley Visitors Bureau, (800)
    458-4748 or (717) 743-7234.

Greater Harrisburg Arts Festival

Harrisburg, Pa., Memorial Day weekend.

Now more than 25 years old, the Greater Harrisburg Arts Festival
hosts about 250 artisans from across the country. Their work includes
virtually all media—photography, woodwork, painting, jewelry, sculpture, glass, and fabric. Each year the festival schedules entertainment
on one or two stages, and strolling oompah bands, puppeteers, drum-
and-bugle brigades, and folk singers join the crowds visiting the arts
and crafts booths. A food court offers Mexican, Middle Eastern, Italian,
and other ethnic specialties. The festival runs through each day of
Memorial Day weekend.

Admission: free.
Location: Fischer Plaza, on the east side of the state capitol.

Information: Greater Harrisburg Arts Council, (717) 238-5180.
Tourist Information: Harrisburg-Hershey-Carlisle Convention
and Visitors Bureau, (717) 232-1377.

Jambalaya Jam

Philadelphia, Pa., Memorial Day weekend.

On Memorial Day weekend, New Orleans comes to Philadelphia.
Four stages feature the best of jazz, zydeco, Cajun, rhythm and
blues, gospel, and Dixieland. Past performers have included Pete
Fountain, the Preservation Hall Jazz Band, Rockin' Dopsie and
the Zydeco Twisters, Beausoleil, and the Olympia Brass Band. A
Junior Jam for children includes special performances, junior
Mardi Gras parades, musical workshops, and mask and jewelry
making. Louisiana craftspeople sell jewelry, masks, and even
voodoo dolls. And, of course, vendors serve plenty of French Quarter favorites, such as seafood gumbo, blackened chicken po'boys,
Cajun shrimp salad, gazpacho, and red beans with andouille
sausage and rice. The festival runs through the afternoon and
evening on Saturday, Sunday, and Memorial Day.

Admission: adults, $10; children ages 2–12, $1; advance ticket
rates.
Location: Penn's Landing.
Information: Jambalaya Jam, (215) 636-1666.
Tourist Information: Philadelphia Convention and Visitors
Bureau, (800) 321-9563 or (215) 636-1666.

Pittsburgh Folk Festival

Pittsburgh, Pa., Memorial Day weekend.

"Unity in diversity" is the theme of the Pittsburgh Folk Festival,
which has presented the music, dance, customs, and foods of
many nations since 1956. Each year about 20 ethnic groups are
invited to demonstrate their customs on stage, set up a display,
and prepare full menus of their native cuisine. In a past festival,

for instance, a Croatian group offered a meal of roast lamb with bread and onions, stuffed cabbage, cabbage and noodles, cheese crepes, and apple strudel. They also set up a display of harvest tools and customs, and performed their native masquerade procession. A Vietnamese group cooked grilled chicken, stir-fried chicken with broccoli, and vegetable fried rice, and performed the traditional Vietnamese wedding ceremony.

The festival also includes an International Bazaar, where items such as wood carvings, textiles, jewelry, clothing, and wall hangings are sold. Children's performances are scheduled Saturday and Sunday afternoon, and a special children's area offers opportunities for children to learn paper-cutting, folk dancing, and egg coloring, or enjoy strolling musicians or a puppet show. The Pittsburgh Folk Festival runs Friday evening and Saturday and Sunday afternoon and evening.

Admission: adults, $6; children ages 6–12, $2; children under 6, free; advance tickets available.

Location: David L. Lawrence Convention Center.

Information: Pittsburgh Folk Festival, (412) 227-6812.

Tourist Information: Pittsburgh Convention and Visitors Bureau, (800) 366-0093 or (412) 281-7711.

Virginia

Heart of Virginia Festival

Farmville, Va., first Saturday in May.

The Heart of Virginia Festival nearly fills the town of Farmville and is divided into three sections. The Country Festival near the Courthouse features country crafts, foods, and entertainment that includes country-and-western bands, gospel singers, and square dancers. The Uptown Festival offers an outdoor art show, gourmet foods, and jazz performances. There have also been Indian dancing, Virginia Piedmont a cappella singing, and a group of retired railroad workers who hammer spikes while singing work songs. The third section of the festival is the Children's Festival, with puppets, clowns, storytelling, and magic. The Heart of Virginia Festival runs from morning until night and also includes a breakfast buffet, an air show, batteau rides, and a fireworks show.

Admission: free.
Location: downtown Farmville and the grounds of Longwood College.
Information: Farmville Chamber of Commerce, (804) 392-3939.

Shenandoah Apple Blossom Festival

Winchester, Va., first weekend in May.

In early May the hillside orchards surrounding Winchester are awash with pink and white blossoms. The town celebrates spring and the blooming of the apple trees with the Shenandoah Apple Blossom Festival, first held in 1924. The traditional highlight of the festival is the coronation of Queen Shenandoah, who is the daughter of a nationally recognized person. Among the past queens have been Susan Ford and Lucy Johnson during their fathers' presidencies, Melissa Rosenberg, daughter of Joan Rivers, and Candace Savalas, daughter of Telly Savalas.

The festival runs from Thursday through Sunday. After the coronation on Friday, the Firefighters' Parade—one of the two parades of the festival—displays more than 250 pieces of firefighting equipment, firefighters from many states, and more than a hundred marching bands. Attracting 250,000 spectators, the Grand Feature Parade on Saturday afternoon is led by a celebrity grand marshal. Lucille Ball, Bob Hope, and Bing Crosby have done the honors in past years. There are more than 20 other events, including dances, band competitions, the Clyde Beatty-Cole Brothers Circus, and a 10-kilometer run.

Admission: varies according to event.
Locations: downtown mall, park, and shopping enter.
Information: Shenandoah Apple Blossom Festival, Inc., (703) 662-3863.
Tourist Information: Winchester-Frederick County Visitors Center, (703) 662-4118.

Whitetop Mountain Ramp Festival

Whitetop, Va., third Sunday in May.

Ramps, or wild leeks, are one of the first spring plants of the Appalachians. Rural people of West Virginia, Virginia, and points south anxiously await the ramps' appearance, when they hike into the woods, dig up the plants, and return home to fry them up with ham and potatoes. The tradition, in fact, began hundreds of years ago when the English settled in Appalachia. They named the plant after a related species in the British Isles commonly known as ramson. Ramson, "son of ram," was named for its appearance during the sign of Aries, March 20 to April 20.

Whitetop is a small town in the mountains of southern Virginia. On a Sunday in May the fire company holds a ramp feed, serving a dinner of barbecued chicken, fried potatoes with ramps, green beans, a roll, and drink. Ramp eaters are entertained through the afternoon with bluegrass, country, gospel, and old-time mountain music. The highlight of the day, though, is the annual Ramp Eating Contest. The festival also includes arts and crafts and children's activities.

Admission: adults, $3; children ages 6–12, $1; children under 6, free; charge for dinner.

Location: Mt. Rogers Fire Hall.

Directions: From Abingdon, Virginia, follow U.S. Route 58 east for 34 miles.

Information: Whitetop Mountain Ramp Festival, (703) 388-3283.

Tourist Information: Virginia Southwest Blue Ridge Highlands, Inc., (703) 431-4300.

Roanoke's Festival in the Park

Roanoke, Va., Thursday before Memorial Day to following weekend.

Roanoke's biggest festival runs for 11 days at Elmwood, Wasena, and Smith parks and other locations in the city. Most activities are held on the two weekends and include all-day entertainment, food, and children's activities at Elmwood Park. In the past, musical entertainment has included jazz, rhythm and blues, rock, country and western, folk, and bluegrass. Special effort is directed toward children's activities, which have included the Backyard Circus (where children dress up and join the act), a marionette show, a children's parade, and hands-on activities like face painting, chalk art, and crafts. During the week there are special concerts at Victory Stadium; performers have included top names such as the Marshall Tucker Band and local talent. Among other events are softball tournaments, a juried crafts show, and the River Race, where a hundred barely riverworthy craft race on the Roanoke River.

Admission: free, except for a $2 festival button for major concerts.
Location: various locations in the Roanoke Valley.
Information: Festival in the Park, (703) 342-2640.
Tourist Information: Roanoke Valley Convention and Visitors Bureau, (703) 342-6025.

West Virginia

Webster County Woodchopping Festival
Webster Springs, W.Va., week before Memorial Day.

Lumberjacks from as far as Australia and England come to the mountain town of Webster Springs to try for the title of World Champion Woodchopper. The event includes competitions in cross-cut sawing, power sawing, and horizontal and vertical woodchopping. Draft-horse-team competitions, the West Virginia State Turkey Calling Contest, a horseshoe-pitching contest, square dancing, country music concerts, and a Grand Feature Parade are also scheduled during the Saturday and Sunday of Memorial Day weekend. Log-loading competitions, athletic tournaments, and bluegrass and country-and-western concerts are held during the preceding week.

Admission: $2.
Location: Baker's Island, Court Square, and other locations in Webster Springs.

Cross-cut saw competition at the Webster County Woodchopping Festival.

Information: Webster County Woodchopping Festival, (304) 847-7666.

Tourist Information: Pocahontas County Tourism Commission, (800) 336-7009 or (304) 799-4636.

Three Rivers Coal Festival

Fairmont, W.Va., Memorial Day Weekend.

Fairmont is in the heart of West Virginia's coal country and celebrates that heritage with a Memorial Day weekend festival. Activities include the coronation of the Festival Queen and Little Miss, cruises on the river aboard the Gateway Clipper, musical performances, a baby contest, a canoe race, the Anything That Floats Contest, a teen dance, and a carnival. Music has included a country jamboree, a battle of the bands, a bluegrass festival, and a gospel show. The Head-of-the-Mon-River Horseshoe Tournament, with world champion horseshoe pitchers competing, also takes place in Fairmont during the weekend.

Admission: free.
Location: Palatine Park.
Information: Three Rivers Coal Festival, (304) 363-2625.
Tourist Information: Marion County Convention and Visitors
   Bureau, (800) 834-7365 or (304) 363-7037.

Vandalia Gathering

*Charleston, W.Va., Friday through Sunday of Memorial
Day weekend.*

The Vandalia Gathering celebrates West Virginia's traditional
and ethnic arts, including music, dance, storytelling, and Appalachian crafts. The event kicks off with a concert Friday evening
and ends Sunday evening with an awards ceremony and another
concert, which usually features the Morris Brothers. In between,
competitions and entertainment appear on three stages Saturday
and Sunday afternoon, and traditional and ethnic dancing is
performed in the Cultural Center great hall, which is hung with
more than 30 quilts. A Craft Circle around the Capitol Fountain
features a selection of Appalachian craftspeople selling and demonstrating their work in pottery, stained glass, weaving, soft-
sculpture dolls, and blacksmithing. Food Row is made up of booths
of community groups selling ethnic and mountain food of the
state.

One highlight of the Vandalia Gathering is the Liars' Contest,
which rewards the storyteller who can spin the most outrageous
yarn. There are also competitions in fiddle, banjo, and lap dulcimer, which bring together traditional musicians from all over
West Virginia. The festival's master musicians and regular performers include Melvin Wine, Wilson Douglas, Aunt Jenny Wilson, and Elmer Bird. The Division of Culture and History even
sends a vehicle to some remote areas to fetch musicians, such as
octogenarian banjo player Sylvie O'Brien, who could not make the
trip on their own. Often these musicians gather for after-hours
jam sessions under the trees and in the backs of pickup trucks.
Admission: free.
Location: Capitol Complex.

Information: Division of Culture and History, (304) 348-0220.
Tourist Information: Charleston Convention and Visitors
Bureau, (800) 733-5469 or (304) 344-5075.

West Virginia Strawberry Festival

Buckhannon, W.Va., week in late May.

During the Great Depression, a group of men in Buckhannon
organized a strawberry festival to promote the crop in the eco-
nomically distressed area. Today, the strawberry is a major crop
in Upshur County, and the week-long West Virginia Strawberry
Festival attracts more than 100,000 people. Among the highlights
of the festival are the marching-band competition and the Grand
Feature Parade, one of the best festival parades in the country.
The festival organizers seek out and invite top marching bands
from across the country, and bands have come from as far away
as California and Texas.

Activities are scheduled all day long most of the week. Visitors
enjoy strawberry shortcake, three large parades, a juried art
show, a fiddle and banjo jamboree, square dancing, a sweetest
strawberry contest, street entertainment, chicken barbecues, country-and-western concerts, and the coronation of the Strawberry
King and Queen. The festival has included a block party with
salsa, conga, and bluegrass music and a block-long strawberry
shortcake.

Admission: free.
Location: in town and Upshur County.
Information: West Virginia Strawberry Festival Association,
(304) 472-9036.
Tourist Information: Buckhannon-Upshur Chamber of
Commerce, (304) 472-1722.

June

Delaware

Greek Festival

Wilmington, Del., first week of June.

Moussaka, pasticcio, souvlakia, gyros, and sweets like baklava and loukoumades are some of the Greek foods served at Wilmington's Greek Festival. Holy Trinity Greek Orthodox Church keeps the event truly ethnic, and only Greek music is performed during the four days. Past entertainers have included the Terpsichorean Dance Troupe, Paul Kauriga and his Orchestra, and the group Poseidon. The festival runs afternoons and evenings Wednesday through Saturday and also offers a Greek coffee shop, games, Sondeen the Clown, and souvenirs.

Admission: free.
Location: Holy Trinity Greek Orthodox Church, 808 N. Broom Street.
Information: Holy Trinity Greek Orthodox Church, (302) 654-4446.
Tourist Information: Greater Wilmington Convention and Visitors Bureau, (800) 422-1181 or (302) 652-4088.

St. Anthony's Italian Festival

Wilmington, Del., second week in June.

One of Wilmington's biggest festivals is the Italian Festival at St. Anthony's Church. Some 330,000 people show up for the week-long event, which features continuous performances of Italian and American music on several outdoor stages. Of course there is lots of good food, including homemade spezzato, mozzarella sticks, chicken cacciatore, handmade cannoli, fresh fruit in wine, Italian pastries, espresso, and cappuccino. Spaghetti and ravioli dinners are served each evening. The festival also offers a midway, raffles, and a feast-day religious celebration and procession of the saints through the neighboring streets of Wilmington's Italian section. The festival runs evenings during the week and midafternoon and evenings on the weekends.

Admission: free.

Location: St. Anthony of Padua Roman Catholic Church, Ninth and du Pont streets.

Information: St. Anthony's Italian Festival, (302) 421-3747.

Tourist Information: Greater Wilmington Convention and Visitors Bureau, (800) 422-1181 or (302) 654-4088.

Accordion orchestra at St. Anthony's Italian Festival.

Maryland and the District of Columbia

Delmarva Chicken Festival

1992: Salisbury, Md., 1993: Cambridge, Md., one weekend in June.

The Delmarva Chicken Festival's 10-foot-wide frying pan cooks up 800 chicken quarters at a time, holds 160 gallons of oil, and is tended by cooks with garden rakes. The lightly seasoned chicken served with applesauce and a roll is the most popular meal at the festival, but barbecued chicken and various ethnic chicken dishes are also available. On even years, a chicken cook-off tests the recipes of chicken cooks; the winners go to the National Chicken Cook-off in Dallas, Texas.

The Delmarva Chicken Festival is held on a weekend in June on the Delmarva Peninsula of Delaware, Maryland, and Virginia, but the specific location changes each year. Entertainment includes performances of bluegrass, country and western, oldies, and light rock. At the Chicken Capers, children can test their skill at tossing eggs, carrying an egg on a spoon through an obstacle course, or digging for money in a pile of cornmeal. The festival also offers a parade, carnival rides, and exhibits.

Admission: free.
Location: changes each year; call for information.
Information: Delmarva Poultry Industry, Inc., (302) 856-9037.
Tourist Information: Wicomico County Tourism, (410) 548-4914; Dorcester County Tourism, (410) 228-1000.

Cypress Festival

Pocomoke City, Md., first weekend following the first day of summer.

Pocomoke City lies on the Pocomoke River, a swift and deep tidal stream now protected as a wild and scenic river. Here on the banks of the river, in one of the country's northernmost stands of cypress, the town celebrates summer, the river, and the famous cypress trees. Running Friday evening and all day Saturday, the festival features performances by local groups, including bluegrass bands, square dancers, bagpipers, and rock groups. Local civic organizations serve up Delmarvelous chicken, raw oysters, crab cakes, and other Eastern Shore specialties. On Saturday, the Pocomoke River Canoe Challenge tests canoeists and kayakers on a 12-mile course down the river, finishing at Cypress Park.

Admission: free.

Location: Cypress Park.

Information: Pocomoke City Chamber of Commerce, (410) 957-1919.

Tourist Information: Worcester County Tourism, (410) 632-3617.

Andean musician at the Smithsonian's Festival of American Folklife.

Tilghman Seafood Festival

Tilghman, Md., last Saturday in June.

The fishing village of Tilghman Island serves up some of the Chesapeake Bay's bounty, including soft crabs, steamed crabs, crab cakes, and steamed clams, all prepared the Tilghman Island way. The day features the crowning of the fire department queen, a parade through Tilghman, country-and-western performances, carnival rides, a crab-picking contest, and a crab race. The Tilghman Seafood Festival runs through Saturday afternoon and evening.

Admission: free.
Location: fire station.
Information: Tilghman Island Volunteer Fire Department, (410) 886-2677.
Tourist Information: Talbot County Tourism, (410) 822-4606.

The Smithsonian's Festival of American Folklife

Washington, D.C., last weekend in June and first weekend in July, including July 4.

The Festival of American Folklife is both a festival and a museum exhibit, offering interesting foods, craft demonstrations, music, and dance—all carefully prepared to educate as much as to entertain. Like a museum, the craft booths, dance stages, and exhibits are organized so that visitors can walk from one to the next, and each station includes a sign explaining what is presented. Visitors enjoy such things as Dixieland bands, Pennsylvania Dutch cooking, Indonesian dancers, Mexican weavers, Appalachian storytellers, and midwestern square dancers.

The festival runs each afternoon Wednesday through Sunday and offers music, dance, lectures, and demonstrations at several locations on the National Mall. One area is devoted to a state or region of the United States. Another focuses on a foreign country and brings in scores of dancers, musicians, cooks, and craftspeople

from that country. Other areas present programs on themes such
as American talkers, music of popular movements, and native
American cultures. Some evenings there are dance parties and
special celebrations. Each year, a million and a half people attend
the folklife festival.

Admission: free.
Location: National Mall.
Information: Smithsonian Visitor Information, (202) 357-2700.
Tourist Information: Washington, D.C., Convention and Visitors
Association, (202) 789-7000.

New Jersey

Hungarian Festival of New Brunswick
New Brunswick, N.J., first Saturday in June.

New Brunswick's Hungarian Festival begins with the ringing of
church bells in the city's Hungarian neighborhood. Known as the
most Hungarian city in the United States, New Brunswick has a
sizeable Hungarian-American population, more than a dozen
Hungarian civic, religious, and cultural organizations, and several churches where Sunday services are still conducted in Hungarian.

Hungarian food and entertainment are provided along Somerset
Street through the afternoon and evening. Chicken paprikesh,
pecsenye and kolbasz (sausages) sandwiches, kalacs, palacsinta
(crepes), langos (fried dough), and kifli (almond crescents) are
some of the dishes served. The women of the Bayard Street
Presbyterian Church sell their homemade noodles, including csiga
(small soup noodles), szeles (wide noodles), metelt (very fine
noodles), and oszva visza (cabbage noodles). The women's group
has been making noodles for 55 years, and the festival is one of
the rare times they sell to the general public.

The Kara-Csubak Radio Orchestra generally plays through the
afternoon. Other stages feature Hungarian folk dancing, including performances by the Hungarian Scouts Folk Dance Ensemble.
Other entertainment has included songs by the children of St.

Ladislaus School, fencing demonstrations by the Hungarian American Athletic Club, and music and dancing in the evening.

Admission: free.

Location: Somerset Street between Bethany and Division streets.

Information: American Hungarian Foundation, (908) 846-5777.

Tourist Information: New Brunswick Chamber of Commerce, (908) 545-4800.

Heritage Days Festival

Trenton, N.J., first weekend in June.

Trenton's Heritage Days celebrates the city's varied ethnic heritage. Nearly 200,000 people attend the weekend event, which features food and drink of many nations and continuous entertainment on four stages. On Trenton Commons and near the stage in Mill Hill Park, vendors and community groups sell all types of ethnic food, including Filipino, Greek, Jamaican, Italian, African, Hispanic, Pakistani, Turkish, German, Korean, and Polish specialties. Entertainment ranges from German oompah music to the blues, from demonstrations of kung fu to native American dancing, from jug bands to classical quintets.

Admission: free.

Location: Mill Hill Park and Trenton Commons.

Information: Trenton Downtown Association, (609) 393-8998.

Tourist Information: Mercer County Chamber of Commerce, (609) 393-4143.

New Jersey Seafood Festival

Belmar, N.J., second Saturday in June.

Shrimp kabob cocktail, clams on the half shell, shrimp eggroll, fried calamari rings, New England seafood chowder, swordfish kabobs, steamed lobster, shrimp cocktail, Cajun crawfish, fried oysters, grilled tuna steaks, mussels marinara, and soft-shelled crab sandwiches: these are some of the seafood treats Jersey Shore restaurants cook up at the New Jersey Seafood Festival.

The good food is accompanied by musical performances, educational exhibits, arts and crafts, and special children's activities like storytelling, clamshell tossing contests, and stunt-kite-flying demonstrations. The festival runs Saturday morning and afternoon.

Admission: free.
Location: Fifth Avenue and the Oceanfront.
Information: Belmar Chamber of Commerce, (908) 681-6006.
Tourist Information: Monmouth County Department of Tourism, (908) 431-7476.

Garden State Winegrowers Spring Festival

Alternating locations in New Jersey, Father's Day weekend.

New Jersey's 15 wineries make it the thirteenth largest winegrowing state, producing 250,000 gallons each year. The wineries bottle champagnes, dessert wines, semidry wines, red wines, and white wines. On Father's Day weekend many of the wineries participate in a spring festival, offering tasting and sales. The admission fee buys a commemorative glass for tasting, and the festival offers musical entertainment, food, and a variety of activities like grape stomping contests, cooking with wine presentations, and wine-making demonstrations. The festival runs Saturday and Sunday afternoon.

Admission: $7.50.
Location: at one of New Jersey's wineries.
Information: New Jersey Wine Industry Advisory Council, (609) 984-9463.
Tourist Information: New Jersey Division of Travel and Tourism, (800) 537-7397.

New Jersey Fresh Seafood Festival

Atlantic City, N.J., third weekend after Memorial Day.

A highlight of the New Jersey Fresh Seafood Festival is the New Jersey Seafood Challenge. Top chefs from all over the state compete, each preparing a "signature" seafood entrée with appropriate appetizers and side courses. The judges—who include restaurant critics, professors of culinary arts, and master chefs—rate the dishes on eight different criteria, including innovation and originality, utilization of ingredients, preparation, cleanliness, and timing. The winner goes on to the American Seafood Challenge, an event that evolved from a 1984 wager between the governors of Virginia and Florida on which state makes the best seafood chowder.

The dishes entered in the New Jersey Seafood Challenge (and perhaps the best seafood chowder) are among the seafood specialties offered during the New Jersey Fresh Seafood Festival. The festival benefits various causes, so commercial fishermen donate their catch and the Professional Chefs Association of South Jersey cooks it up. Two stages provide continuous entertainment, including variety acts, beach music bands, jazz groups, and local singers. The festival is held during National Fishing Week and runs all day Saturday and Sunday.

Admission: $2.

Location: Historic Gardner's Basin, at North New Hampshire Avenue and the bay.

Information: Greater Atlantic City Convention and Visitors Bureau, (609) 348-7100.

New York

Lower East Side Jewish Festival

New York, N.Y., Sunday in June.

New York's Lower East Side is known as the original home of Eastern European Jewish immigrants, with settlements there before 1776. A local cemetery, in fact, contains the graves of 18 Jewish soldiers who fought in the revolutionary war. At one time the neighborhood contained 350,000 Jewish people and nearly 500 synagogues. The Lower East Side was home to the Yiddish Theatre and to such luminaries as Eddie Cantor, Molly Picon, and Zero Mostel.

Since 1976, the Jewish community has celebrated its heritage with a Sunday of music, folk dancing, and kosher foods. Past performers have included Schlomo Carlebach, Yoel Schrabi, Avram Pengas and the Noga Band, Elam Mamber, Joe Elias and the Ladino Singers, and Westend Klezmania. Vendors sell such things as Judaica art, ceramics, candles, Jewish ritual objects, and puppets. The festival runs from late morning to early evening, with performances through the afternoon.

Admission: free.
Location: East Broadway from Essex Street to Clinton Street.
Information: The Educational Alliance, Inc., (212) 475-6200.
Tourist Information: New York Convention and Visitors Association, (212) 397-8222.

Ithaca Festival

Ithaca, N.Y., first weekend in June.

On Cayuga Lake, Ithaca celebrates the performing and visual arts in early June. The highlight of the event is the almost continuous performances on several stages. Friday is Children's Day on Ithaca Commons, with puppeteers, school choruses, clowns, sea chantey singers, and storytellers performing through the day. On Saturday, six stages offer reggae, progressive rock, jazz, Celtic music, poetry readings, music of the Andes, a cappella, bluegrass, and barbershop quartets. Dance troupes perform ballet, tap, modern, and ethnic dances. Often unusual programs are scheduled, such as experimental music with New Age orchestrations, choral arrangements, and synthesizers. On Sunday, the festival moves to Stewart Park on the lake for a grand finale, with a day of mostly rock and popular music on three stages. Throughout the festival, vendors sell a variety of foods, including falafel, pesto pizza, barbecue sandwiches, Navajo fried bread, chicken curries, potato pancakes, and gourmet sausages.

Admission: free.
Location: Stewart Park and the Commons.
Information: Ithaca Festival, (607) 273-3646.

Tourist Information: Ithaca-Tompkins County Convention and
Visitors Bureau, (800) 284-8422 or (607) 272-1313.

Riverfest

Poughkeepsie, N.Y., first weekend in June.

Poughkeepsie welcomes spring with an outdoor festival on the
banks of the Hudson River. Continuous entertainment is provided on two stages throughout the weekend, and past performers
have included the Greg Allman Band, Southside Johnny, Larry
Carlton, and the Hudson Valley Philharmonic. There are also
karate demonstrations, drum and bugle corps performances, a
petting zoo, a local history fair, carnival rides, and a fireworks
show Sunday night. Organizations and commercial vendors sell
Italian, German, Tex-Mex, and American food. The festival runs
Saturday and Sunday afternoon and evening.

Admission: free.

Location: Delaval property at the foot of Pine Street and Rinaldi
Boulevard.

Information: WPDH Radio, (914) 471-1500.

Tourist Information: Dutchess County Tourism, (800) 445-3131
or (914) 229-0033.

Miller Balloon Festival

Jamesville, N.Y., weekend in early June.

Soon after the first light of dawn, more than 40 colorful hot-air
balloons quietly rise over Jamesville Beach Park. The scene is
repeated, morning and evening, during the weekend of the Miller
Balloon Festival. Crowds gather to watch the balloon launches
and races and to enjoy amusement rides, stage entertainment,
and parachute jumps. The food is plentiful and includes spiedies,
barbecued pork, ice cream sundaes, and, of course, Miller beer.
The Land of Oz Family Activity Center gives kids a chance to hop
in a real balloon basket, make a kite, or sing along with folk
entertainers.

Admission: adults, $2; children ages 5–14, $1; children under 5, free.
Location: Jamesville Beach Park.
Directions: from Syracuse, take I-481 to exit 2; then go south on Route 91 to Jamesville; turn right on Route 173, then left on Jamesville Apulia Road.
Information: Onondaga County Parks, (315) 451-7275.
Tourist Information: Syracuse-Onondaga Convention and Visitors Bureau, (800) 234-4797 or (315) 470-1800.

Allentown Outdoor Art Festival
Buffalo, N.Y., second full weekend in June.

Since 1957 the Victorian Allentown neighborhood of Buffalo has been the setting for a weekend spring arts festival. More than 450 exhibitors from all over the country participate in the juried show. They line the streets of Allentown, showing and selling their work in painting, photography, sculpture, jewelry, glasswork, wood, fabric, leather, and many other media. Vendors and community groups sell festival food, and strolling performers entertain the crowds. Allentown is one of the nation's largest preservation districts and contains several historic sites, including the location where Teddy Roosevelt was inaugurated after McKinley was shot.

Admission: free.
Location: Allentown district.
Information: Allentown Village Society, (716) 881-4269.
Tourist Information: Greater Buffalo Convention and Visitors Bureau, (800) 283-3256 or (716) 852-0511.

Feast of St. Anthony
New York, N.Y., 11 days in mid-June.

St. Anthony's Church in Greenwich Village is the national shrine of St. Anthony, a priest in Padua, Italy, who died in 1231. Each year the church holds an 11-day festival around June 13, St. Anthony's feast day. The festival draws thousands for Italian food, Italian music, rides for kids, and games of chance. Sullivan Street is lined with booths selling cannoli, chicken cacciatore, ravioli, sausages and peppers, espresso, and other Italian treats. Opera singers, accordion players, and Italian orchestras entertain the crowds. On the feast day, a procession carries a statue of the saint through the neighborhood streets.

Admission: free.

Location: Sullivan Street between West Houston and Spring streets.

Information: St. Anthony's Church, (212) 777-2755.

Tourist Information: New York Convention and Visitors Association, (212) 397-8222.

Welcome Back to Brooklyn

Brooklyn, N.Y., Sunday in mid-June.

Brooklynites everywhere return to their hometown for Welcome Back to Brooklyn, an annual street festival with Brooklyn entertainment, food, crafts, and games. The festival kicks off at noon with the Children's Neighborhood Parade led by the King of Brooklyn, a hometown boy done well. Past kings have included Jimmy Smits, Louis Gossett Jr., Ben Vereen, and Henny Youngman. The festival stretches along a mile of Eastern Parkway, with rows of food vendors, craftspeople demonstrating their work, and athletic demonstrations by Brooklyn champions.

At the Games Arcade festivalgoers can try hopscotch, skelly, jacks, and other street games. The variety of food served reflects the diversity of Brooklyn and includes such famous Brooklyn treats as Nathan's Hot Dogs and Junior's Cheesecake. Activities through the afternoon include the induction of baseball stars into the Brooklyn Dodgers Hall of Fame, children's storytelling and activities, and entertainment on a number of stages. Past acts have included Roots of Brazil, Dairaba West Afrikan Dance Company, Young Soon Kim White Wave Rising Dance Company, and Brooklyn Conservatory Jazz Band.

Admission: free.

Location: Eastern Parkway from Grand Army Plaza to

Washington Avenue, Brooklyn.

Information: New York Convention and Visitors Bureau, (212) 397-8222.

Riverfest

Scotia, N.Y., third Saturday in June.

Over 100 decorated watercraft ply the Mohawk River for the daytime boat parade at Riverfest. Competing skippers vie for awards in categories such as most creative, most beautiful, most unusual, and most comical. At night, another parade features 20 luxury cruisers, each decorated with hundreds of electric lights. Benefiting the American Red Cross, Riverfest runs through Saturday afternoon and evening and also includes performances by the Bud Lite Water Ski Team, stage entertainment, international foods, and a fireworks display.

Admission: free.

Location: Collins and Freedom Parks.

Information: American Red Cross, Schenectady County Chapter, (518) 393-3606.

Tourist Information: Schenectady County Chamber of Commerce, (800) 962-8007 or (518) 372-5656.

Clearwater's Great Hudson River Revival

Valhalla, N.Y., third weekend in June.

About 25 years ago folksinger Pete Seeger read a book about the great wooden sloops of the Hudson River. The thought occurred to him and some friends to build a replica of a Hudson River sloop and use it not only to teach people about the Hudson River's history but also about the river's serious pollution problem. To raise money for the project, the group put on an afternoon of music called the Hudson Valley Folk Picnic and raised $167. In a few years, however, the annual event grew in popularity, and before long the group launched its 106-foot sloop, the *Clearwater*.

*Stilt walkers at Clearwater's
Great Hudson River Revival.*

Today the *Clearwater* still sails the Hudson, the river is cleaner, and the afternoon folk concert has grown into a two-day musical and cultural event known as the Great Hudson River Revival. More than 60 entertainers perform on six stages on the campus of Westchester Community College. The festival concentrates on American music, such as gospel, bluegrass, blues, and native American songs. Recent revivals have featured Suzanne Vega, Sweet Honey in the Rock, and Peter, Paul and Mary. Strolling jugglers, mimes, and new vaudevillians wander among the crowds; vendors sell a variety of ethnic foods; and environmental groups sponsor exhibits. There is a special area with activities for children, and all entertainment is accessible to the disabled.

Admission: in advance, $22/weekend, $13/day; at gate, $25/weekend, $16/day; over 65 or with disability, $7.50; children 12 and under, free.

Location: Westchester Community College.

Directions: for train connections telephone 1-800-METRO INFO.

Information: Hudson River Sloop Clearwater, Inc., 112 Market Street, Poughkeepsie, NY 12601.

Tourist Information: Westchester County Convention and Visitors Bureau, (914) 948-0047.

Owego Strawberry Festival

Owego, N.Y., third weekend in June.

Strawberry shortcake, strawberry ice cream, Belgian waffles with strawberries, chocolate-covered strawberries, and even strawberry pizza are some of the treats served at Owego's Strawberry Festival. The festival begins Friday evening with a classic rock concert, a strawberry dessert baking contest, and a fireworks show, but most activities are on Saturday, including performances on three stages, a parade, and about 250 vendors selling food, crafts, and antiques. Entertainment has included morris dancers, country-and-western singers, gymnasts, and old-time fiddlers.

Admission: free.
Location: throughout the town.
Information: Owego Strawberry Festival, P.O. Box 425, Owego, NY 13827.
Tourist Information: Tioga County Chamber of Commerce, (607) 687-2020.

Italian Festival

Hunter, N.Y., last weekend in June.

Besides good Italian music and food, Hunter Mountain's Italian Festival features top-name entertainers of Italian heritage, such as Frankie Avalon, Bobby Rydell, and Tony Bennett. The weekend festival is one of Hunter Mountain's most popular, with three afternoons and evenings of performances by entertainers like Julius LaRosa, Joe Mauro, I Paesani, Amici di Campagna, and Cristina Fontanelli. A tent larger than a football field holds the entertainment area, an Italian arts and crafts show, and Italian food and drink concessions.

Admission: adults, $9; children 12 and under, $2; reserved seating tickets may be available.

Location: Hunter Mountain.
Directions: from Catskill, New York, follow Route 23A west for
    21 miles.
Information: Hunter Mountain Festivals, Ltd., (518) 263-3800.
Tourist Information: Greene County Promotion Department,
    (800) 542-2414 or (518) 943-3223.

Pennsylvania

Three Rivers Arts Festival

*Pittsburgh, Pa., starts first Friday in June and runs for 17
days.*

The Three Rivers Arts Festival is Pittsburgh's salute to the performing and visual arts: 17 days of exhibitions, performances, and
cultural activities that take place amid the skyscrapers downtown and at Point State Park where the Allegheny and the
Monongahela join to form the Ohio River. Held since 1960, the
festival now attracts hundreds of thousands of people. In addition
to exhibitions of sculpture, paintings, graphics, fiber art, crafts,
and photography, the festival offers film and video presentations,
an artists' market, and children's activities. Three stages feature
top-name acts as well as local performers.

Admission: free.
Location: downtown and Point State Park.
Information: Three Rivers Arts Festival, (412) 481-7040.
Tourist Information: Pittsburgh Convention and Visitors
    Bureau, (800) 366-0093 or (412) 281-7711.

Susquehanna Boom Festival

*Williamsport, Pa., second Saturday in June until the fol-
lowing weekend.*

In the late 1800s, when Williamsport was the "lumber capital of
the world," the Susquehanna Boom was a seven-mile-long stone

and timber crib that caught logs floating down the West Branch of the Susquehanna River from the forests of north-central Pennsylvania. The branded logs were sorted and moved to the holding ponds of the 35 sawmills in Williamsport. The lumber barons who owned the mills became enormously wealthy, and Williamsport had more millionaires per capita than anywhere else in the world.

The Susquehanna Boom Festival runs from Saturday to Saturday with lunchtime entertainment during the week. The festival generally begins with a parade on Saturday that is followed by a block party with music and dancing. Victorian Sunday features Victorian dress, buggy rides, a strawberry festival, a garden art show, and tours of mansions on Millionaire's Row. The festival ends with the Lumberjacks' Jamboree, which features chopping, sawing, and log-rolling competitions.

Admission: free; charges for some events.
Location: various locations in Williamsport.
Information: Susquehanna Boom Festival Foundation, (800) 358-9900 or (717) 321-1203.
Tourist Information: Lycoming County Tourist Promotion Agency, (800) 358-9900 or (717) 321-1200.

Noxen Rattlesnake Roundup

Noxen, Pa., mid-June.

The big annual event in Noxen, a small village in the mountains of northern Pennsylvania, is the Rattlesnake Roundup. The locals go up into the mountains—turning over stones, checking rocky ledges, pushing back bushes—to catch snakes and bring them back to a fenced-in pen at the festival grounds. At the end of the two-day hunt, prizes go for the largest rattlesnake, the snake with the most rattles, the largest combined length of two snakes, the largest nonpoisonous snake, and the most variety of snake species caught. Snakes are displayed in the pen and then, according to Pennsylvania Fish Commission regulations, released unharmed into the wild.

The festival generally runs in the evening on Thursday and Friday and in the afternoon and evening Saturday and Sunday. Local country bands perform each evening, the firemen hold a

*Snake Handler at the Noxen Rattle-
snake Roundup.*

parade on Friday, and the snakes are brought in and displayed
Saturday and Sunday. As part of the festival, local schoolchildren
compete for the best drawing of a rattlesnake, and the local
postmaster offers a special rattlesnake hunt cancellation using
the winner's artwork.

Admission: free, except $1 for evening performances.
Location: Noxen Volunteer Fire Company grounds.
Information: Lew Hackling, (717) 298-2420.
Tourist Information: Endless Mountains Visitors Bureau, (717)
   836-5431.

Pennsylvania State Laurel Festival

Wellsboro, Pa., third week in June.

Mountain laurel is the state flower of Pennsylvania, and Wellsboro celebrates its blooming in late June. Wellsboro is a small town in the mountains of northern Pennsylvania not far from Pine Creek Gorge, known as "Pennsylvania's Grand Canyon." First held in 1936, the Pennsylvania State Laurel Festival is a week-long event, with a concert series and a firemen's carnival each night. Most activities, though, are on the last Saturday. The Court House Green has arts and crafts, food, and entertainment; the Laurel Parade is in the afternoon; and the Laurel Queen is crowned in the evening.

Admission: free.
Location: the Green and Main Street.
Information: Wellsboro Area Chamber of Commerce, (717) 724-1926.
Tourist Information: Tioga Association for Recreation and Tourism, (800) 332-6718 (in Pa.) or (717) 662-4466.

Delco Scottish Games

Devon, Pa., third Saturday in June.

The Delco Scottish Games have been held for more than 25 years and are one of the largest in the East. The day-long event features husky men in kilts throwing all manner of objects, including long-handled hammers, bags of straw, and 20-foot wooden poles. Bagpipe bands compete in the Champion Supreme Bagpipe Band Competition, and youthful dancers vie for honors in the Eastern United States Highland Dancing Closed Championship. The Scottish Fair offers woolens, jewelry, bagpipes, and Scottish food like meat pies, fish and chips, and scones. The festival also includes a massed pipe band performance, an Open Piobaireachd (individual bagpipe-playing) Competition, and a whiskey-tasting party.

Admission: adults, $8; children ages 6–14, $3; children under 6 free.

Location: Devon Horse Show Grounds, U.S. Route 30.
Directions: Devon is a stop on the Paoli local train; the show
grounds are a block from the station.
Information: Delco Scottish Games Association, (215) 825-4381.
Tourist Information: Valley Forge Convention and Visitors
Bureau, (800) 441-3549 or (215) 278-3558.

Patch Town Days

Eckley, Pa., Father's Day weekend.

In the anthracite coal fields of northeastern Pennsylvania, coal
companies built simple towns at each mine. Called "patch towns,"
they consisted of rows of nearly identical frame houses for the
miners, a company store, and a breaker, or coal processing plant.
Eckley, one of these patch towns, is now owned and run by the
Pennsylvania Historical Museum as a living museum, and retired
miners, widows, and their children still live in unpainted clap-
board homes. Eckley also provided the setting for the 1970 film
The Molly Maguires, starring Sean Connery.

Patch Town Days celebrates mining life of a century ago.
Blacksmiths, tinsmiths, shoemakers, needle workers, and other
period craftspeople demonstrate and sell their work. Entertainment has included the Lithuanian singing group Sodauto, the
Ukrainian folk ensemble Kazka, Dr. B. B. Bumstead's Lenape
Liquid Show, and the Stephen Foster Singers. The ethnic history
of the patch towns is also represented in the festival's food, such
as German wurst and lieberkase, Lithuanian haluskie and halupki,
Polish pierogi, and Slovak nut rolls and poppyseed rolls.

Admission: adults, $4; senior citizens, $3; children $1.
Location: Eckley Miners' Village.
Directions: from Hazelton follow Pennsylvania Route 940 north
to Jeddo; turn right on road to Eckley.
Information: Eckley Miners' Village, (717) 636-2070.
Tourist Information: Pocono Mountains Vacation Bureau, (800)
762-6667 or (717) 424-6050.

Punxsutawney Groundhog Festival

Punxsutawney, Pa., last full week of June.

Punxsutawney, Pennsylvania, is the home of Punxsutawney Phil, the official groundhog who on February 2 either sees his shadow or doesn't—and thus determines the arrival of spring. The town waits until the arrival of summer, though, to hold its Groundhog Festival, a week-long event with a frog jumping contest, donkey races, a magic circus, and an Appalachian Wagon Train parade among the usual activities. On the two weekends, when the major events are scheduled, groups such as the Punxsy Local 624 Big Dance Band and Punxsy Phil-Harmonyck Symphonette perform at Barclay Square. Civic groups offer pig roasts, bake-offs, food fests, and concessions at various times throughout the week. Phil will be in the Groundhog Zoo at the civic complex, of course, and festivalgoers can visit his official home, Gobbler's Knob, on the edge of town.

Admission: free.
Location: various locations in and around Punxsutawney.
Information: Punxsutawney Groundhog Festival Committee, (814) 938-7687.
Tourist Information: The Magic Forests of West Central Pennsylvania, (800) 348-9393 or (814) 849-5197.

Erie Summer Festival of the Arts

Erie, Pa., last full weekend in June.

Erie's largest art festival features work of all kinds, including music, drama, poetry, painting, and sculpture. During the three-day festival, evening performances on the main stage feature everything from classical to bluegrass, rock to Latino, solo to ensemble. Past performers have included Spyro Gyra, the Paul Winter Consort, Bill Miller, and Livingston Taylor. A second stage offers a variety of music throughout the day. The Panorama fine arts show features works of regional artists and a special area where artists and craftspeople demonstrate their techniques.

Another area offers children's entertainment and opportunities for children to create art of their own.

Admission: free.

Location: Villa Maria Campus of Gannon University.

Information: Erie Summer Festival, (814) 871-7336.

Tourist Information: Tourist and Convention Bureau of Erie County, (814) 454-7191.

Snake Hunt and Rattlesnake Sacking Contest

Cross Fork, Pa., last full weekend in June.

At the Pennsylvania State Rattlesnake Sacking Competition, sponsored by the Keystone Reptile Club, snakes are dumped out of cloth bags and teams consisting of a bagger and a handler are judged on how fast they can recapture their snake and get it back into the bag. Pennsylvania Fish Commission rules prevent the competition from using the native timber rattlers, so Texas diamondbacks are brought in. The event even includes a family sacking contest—but with nonpoisonous snakes. Qualifying contests are held Saturday afternoon, and the championship takes place Sunday afternoon.

For the snake hunt, hunters comb the mountains surrounding Cross Fork, bringing back the snakes they find to a pen at the fire company grounds. Prizes are awarded for the biggest rattler, the snake with the most rattles, and the biggest copperhead snake. The weekend also includes a Saturday firefighters' parade, a firefighters' water battle, a greased pig chase for the kids, talks and exhibits by the Keystone Reptile Club, a flea market, and breakfasts and dinners served by the fire company.

Admission: free.

Location: Kettle Creek Hose Company grounds.

Directions: Cross Fork is between Galeton and Renovo on Route 144.

Information: Debbie Stone, (717) 923-1428.

Tourist Information: Potter County Recreation, Inc., (814) 435-2290.

Pennsylvania Renaissance Faire

Manheim, Pa., last weekend in June through second weekend in October.

An Elizabethan country festival of the late sixteenth century is recreated on summer and fall weekends at the Mount Hope Estate and Winery in northern Lancaster County. At Bosworth Field, armored knights joust before the Queen's reviewing stand. Visitors and performers become pawns, rooks, knights, and bishops at the Human Chess Match. Professional actors perform Shakespearean drama at the estate's Globe Theatre. Hundreds of authentically costumed entertainers perform at the festival's 11 stages or among the crowds. Foods of old England, such as spitted pig, turkey drumsticks, and ribs of boar, are served at 15 food and drink buildings in the Tudor village.

Admission: adults, $14; children ages 5–11, $4.
Location: Mount Hope Estate and Winery.
Directions: from Exit 20 of the Pennsylvania Turnpike follow Route 72 south for 0.5 mile.
Information: Mount Hope Estate and Winery, (717) 665-7285.
Tourist Information: Pennsylvania Dutch Convention and Visitors Bureau, (800) 735-2629 or (717) 299-8901.

Virginia

Vintage Virginia

Front Royal, Va., first weekend in June.

Vintage Virginia, sponsored by the Virginia Wineries Association, features wines from 35 Virginia wineries, 60 arts and crafts exhibits, entertainment on three stages, wine appreciation seminars, special activities for children, and even grape stomping. Stage entertainment has included New Orleans jazz, folk, rock, and reggae. The Commodores, the U.S. Navy's premier jazz band, usually performs on Sunday afternoon.

The festival runs both Saturday and Sunday afternoons. At the gate, visitors receive a souvenir Vintage Virginia wine glass to use for sampling the many wines. Each winery offers its selection of wines for tasting and also sells bottles and cases. There is plenty of food, including some regional dishes. Located in the foothills of the Blue Ridge, the festival site also offers swimming, canoeing, and picnicking.

Admission: adults, $10 in advance, $12 at the gate; under 21, $2; children under 2, free.

Location: Northern Virginia 4-H Educational Center.

Directions: from the intersection of Route 55 and U.S. Route 522 in Front Royal, follow U.S. Route 522 south 1.7 miles. Turn right onto Route 604 (Harmony Hollow Road) and proceed 2 miles to the 4-H Center.

Information: Virginia Wineries Association, (800) 277-2675.

Tourist Information: Front Royal-Warren County Chamber of Commerce and Visitors Center, (703) 635-3185.

Alexandria Red Cross Waterfront Festival

Alexandria, Va., first full weekend (including Friday) in June.

The Waterfront Festival is Alexandria's largest event and the largest fund-raiser of any Red Cross chapter in the country. Held in Oronoco Bay Park at colonial Alexandria's Potomac River waterfront, the festival often brings visiting tall ships, research ships, and ships of foreign navies, all open for tours.

Continuous entertainment is scheduled for several stages Friday evening, Saturday afternoon and evening, and Sunday afternoon. Headliners have included Eric Burdon and the Bryan Auger Band, and local musicians perform jazz, pop, Carolina beach music, and symphony. Clowns, jugglers, and storytellers entertain on the children's stage. Other activities include arts and crafts, a 10-kilometer run, and fireworks shows.

Admission: adults, $3; children ages 6–12, $1; children under 6, free.

Location: Oronoco Bay Park.

Rock musician Eric Burdon performs at Alexandria's Red Cross Waterfront Festival.

Information: Alexandria Chapter of the American Red Cross, (703) 838-4200 or (703) 549-8300.

Tourist Information: Alexandria Convention and Visitors Bureau, (703) 838-4200.

Seawall Festival

Portsmouth, Va., first full weekend in June.

Portsmouth's Seawall Festival celebrates the city's maritime heritage with a weekend of family fun. From Friday evening until Sunday evening, three stages offer a variety of performances. On the Children's Stage, students from every Portsmouth school participate, demonstrating their talents at baton twirling, dancing, acrobatics, and singing. There are also magicians, jugglers, and clowns. Two stages more oriented to adults feature big-band music, beach music, rhythm and blues, soul, and classic rock and roll. Most performers are well known in the Southeast, and past festivals have featured Fat Ammon's Band, Ernie LeBeau and the

Beach Blasters, Baby Huey and the Babysitters, and 1964: As the Beatles. The festival also offers seafood and festival food, tall ships, and a fireworks show Saturday night.

Admission: free.
Location: Portside area at Portsmouth Harbor.
Information: Ports Events, (804) 393-9933.
Tourist Information: Portsmouth Department of Parks and Recreation, (804) 393-8481.

Harborfest

Norfolk, Va., first full weekend in June.

Every year since the Bicentennial, tall sailing ships have returned to Norfolk's harbor for the city's annual summer celebration of life by the sea. The tall ships, along with 140 other military, civilian, and recreational water craft, kick off the festival midday Friday with a parade of sail from Hampton to Norfolk harbor.

Among the tall ships have been the US *Bear*, a 270-foot, medium-endurance Coast Guard cutter; the *Gazela*, a 177-foot, three-masted schooner that was built in Portugal in 1883; and the *Susan Constant*, a reproduction of one of the three ships that transported 104 British colonists to Virginia in 1607. Many of these tall sailing ships offer tours throughout Harborfest.

More than a million people attend Harborfest, Norfolk's biggest festival. A variety of musical entertainment, including big-band swing, jazz, country and western, and classical, is presented at several stages throughout the three-day event. There are also military demonstrations, such as maneuvers by the U.S. Navy SEALs, as well as sailboat races, aerobatic air shows, children's activities, and a spectacular fireworks display on Saturday night. Scores of booths sell everything from seafood to soul food.

Admission: free.
Location: Point Park, Norfolk's downtown waterfront, and Freemason Harbor neighborhood.
Information: Norfolk Festivents, (804) 627-7809.

Tourist Information: Norfolk Convention and Visitors Bureau, (804) 441-5266.

June Jubilee

Richmond, Va., second weekend in June.

Richmond's annual arts festival brings in a variety of musical entertainment, including folk, country, blues, rock, reggae, rhythm and blues, and gospel. Through the afternoon and evening on both Saturday and Sunday, as many as six stages feature both local and nationally known entertainers. Usually a classic rock group— one year it was Steppenwolf—appears. Other well-known performers have included Bachman Turner Overdrive, the Atlanta Rhythm Section, and Livingston Taylor.

The June Jubilee celebrates and showcases the performing, visual, and culinary arts, and is held in one of Richmond's many interesting neighborhoods. While music is the highlight of the event, the weekend also includes an artists' market, with craftspeople demonstrating their work. The streets are also filled with strolling musicians, mimes, jugglers, and clowns. Vendors sell such things as steak in a sac, deep-fried fish, and kabobs. Often the festival includes special events like a farmers' market or a historic reenactment.

Admission: $3; children 12 and under, free.
Location: varies year to year.
Information: Arts Council of Richmond, (804) 643-4993.
Tourist Information: Metro Richmond Convention and Visitors Bureau, (804) 782-2777.

Festival by the James

Lynchburg, Va., second or third weekend in June.

In the 1700s large flat-bottomed boats plied Virginia's James River, carrying tobacco, flour, iron, and apple brandy downriver to urban markets and returning with such things as harpsichords, millstones, and books for the rural people. These commercial craft, called batteaux, were initially based on the Indian dugout canoe. In 1775, Anthony and Benjamin Rucker invented a new batteau made of sawn lumber with a low draft for the river's swift, shallow water. Within a few years as many as 500 batteaux traveled the James and were the major means of transport in the region.

Lynchburg was one of the batteau stops. During the Festival by the James, recreated batteaux with crews in eighteenth-century clothing put in at Lynchburg, the first stop of the annual James River Batteau Festival. The boats travel down the river for eight days, stopping overnight in communities along the way; each town sponsors evening celebrations with music, dance, and storytelling.

The Festival by the James, running Friday evening through Saturday, also offers two stages of entertainment, which often includes country bands, gospel choirs, folk singers, contemporary rock groups, and storytellers. The festival includes a canoe race, a horse-pull contest, a community market, crafts shows, children's games, and batteau rides.

Admission: free.
Location: at the riverfront.
Information: Festival by the James, (804) 845-2604.
Tourist Information: Lynchburg Department of Economic Development, (804) 847-1654.

Court Days

Woodstock, Va., third weekend in June.

In the old days, county court met in Woodstock, Virginia, only once a month. Court Day not only brought county residents to town for court business, but the fury of activity made it a good time to shop, socialize, and be entertained. Next to the town pump, a patent medicine vendor would stand behind his painted wagon, telling jokes and selling his cure-all potion. On the Court Square, crowds would gather around an organ grinder with his monkey or perhaps a man with a dancing bear.

Woodstock remembers Court Day with a weekend festival. A reenactment of a historical trial is held at Court Square on Saturday. Local musicians square off at the Fiddlin' and Banjo Contest or perform on stage, and there are street dances at night. Other activities include a foot race, historical home tours, children's games, an ice-cream-making contest, and antique autos. The festival generally includes an old-fashioned pig roast and pancake breakfasts on the weekend mornings.

Admission: free.
Location: Main and Court streets.
Information: Woodstock Chamber of Commerce, (703) 459-2542.
Tourist Information: Shenandoah County Economic Development Council, (703) 459-5522.

West Virginia

Ronceverte River Festival

Ronceverte, W.Va., first weekend of June.

On the banks of the Greenbrier River, the Ronceverte River Festival offers a weekend of country contests, tournaments, and races. They include a storytelling contest, a horseshoe tournament, a bicycle race, a firefighters' competition, a USCA-sanctioned canoe race, a big fish contest, a lumberjack contest, and an Anything That Floats But a Boat Race. In the Rubber Ducky Race, the owner of the first rubber ducky to cross the finish line wins $5,000. The festival also features Friday and Saturday evening concerts in the park's amphitheater, street dances, clogging demonstrations, a classic car and street rod show, a classic horse show, a parade, and concessions.

Admission: free, except for special entertainment.
Location: Island Park, 4 miles south of Lewisburg.
Information: Ronceverte River Festival, (304) 645-7911.
Tourist Information: White Sulphur Springs Convention and Visitors Bureau, (800) 284-9440 or (304) 536-9440.

Mountain Heritage Arts and Crafts Festival

Harpers Ferry, W.Va., second full weekend in June.

The Mountain Heritage Arts and Crafts festival is one of West Virginia's biggest crafts festivals, with nearly 200 exhibitors. The festival organizers carefully jury the artisans: each is required to send an actual example of his or her work for review, not just a photograph or sketch. The judges categorize the submissions and invite the top 10 craftspeople in fields such as basketry, clothing, decorative painting, dolls, dried flowers, jewelry, and musical instruments. At the festival, each artisan is required to demonstrate, or at least explain, his or her work. The festival also features country food, special demonstrations, and continuous performances by local and regional musicians, usually of the bluegrass variety. The event runs morning and afternoon Friday, Saturday, and Sunday.

Admission: adults, $4; children ages 6-15, $2.
Location: Mountain Heritage Festival Grounds, Route 220.
Information: Jefferson County Chamber of Commerce, (304) 725-2055 or (800) 624-0577.
Tourist Information: Jefferson County Convention and Visitors Bureau, (304) 535-2627.

July

Delaware

Ice Cream Festival
Wilmington, Del., second full weekend in July.

Wilmington's Ice Cream Festival is a Victorian ice cream social, with entertainment, demonstrations, and refreshments popular at the turn of the century. Homemade ice cream is served with a variety of toppings, including one flavor developed just for the festival. Highwheel bicyclists, organ grinders, a Victorian baby parade, and hot-air balloons are some of the sights on the Rockwood Museum's landscaped grounds. Magicians, storytellers, barbershop quartets, and jugglers perform. A juried Victorian crafts fair includes stained glass, quilting, beadwork, and reverse painting on glass. The festival runs through the afternoon and early evening both Saturday and Sunday.

Admission: adults, $4; seniors, $3; children over 5 years, $1.
Location: Rockwood Museum, 610 Shipley Road.
Information: Rockwood Museum, (302) 571-7776.
Tourist Information: Greater Wilmington Convention and Visitors Bureau, (800) 422-1181 or (302) 652-4088.

Maryland and the District of Columbia

The Smithsonian's Festival of American Folklife

Washington, D.C., last weekend in June, first weekend in July, including July 4.

See June—Maryland and the District of Columbia.

American Indian Inter-Tribal Cultural Organization Powwow

McHenry, Md., weekend following July 4.

The powwow is a social event for native Americans, but the Inter-Tribal Cultural Organization Powwow is one that is open to the general public. The event attracts full-blooded and mixed-blood representatives of more than 30 tribes, including Sioux, Seneca, Mohawk, Cayuga, Cherokee, Apache, and Creek. One event open to the public is intertribal dancing, where drumming and singing groups create the music for many arena dancers in full regalia. There are also demonstrations of specialty dances, such as the hoop dance. Native American artisans demonstrate their work, and vendors sell crafts and foods like frybread and Indian tacos. The powwow runs through the afternoon Friday, Saturday, and Sunday.

Admission: adults, $4; children under 12, free.

Location: Garrett County Fairgrounds, on U.S. Route 219, 13 miles south of U.S. Route 48.

Information: American Indian Inter-Tribal Cultural Organization, Twinbrook Station, P.O. Box 775, Rockville, MD 20848-0775.

Tourist Information: Deep Creek Lake-Garrett County Promotion Council, (301) 334-1948.

*Hoop dancer performs at the
American Indian Inter-Tribal
Cultural Organization Pow-
wow.*

Italian Festival

Baltimore, Md., weekend in middle of July.

The Italian Festival is one of the major events of Baltimore's
Showcase of Nations festival series. Celebrating the heritage of
Baltimore's Italian community, the festival offers three days of
Italian entertainment and food. Past festivals have featured the
Monaldi Brothers, Aldo and the Composers, and the Bali D'Italia
Dance Company. There are events for children featuring comedians, magicians, and puppet shows. The weekend includes games
and contests, such as a pizza-eating contest and a cannoli-eating
contest. There are displays of classic marble work, Italian paintings, and authentic costumes. The festival runs afternoons and
evenings Friday, Saturday, and Sunday.

Admission: adults, $3; children under 12, free with adult.
Location: Festival Hall, Pratt and Sharp streets.

Information: Baltimore Area Visitors Center, (410) 837-4636 or
(800) 282-6632.
Tourist Information: Baltimore Area Convention and Visitors
Association, (410) 659-7300.

Blue Bayou Music Festival

Upper Marlboro, Md., second Saturday in July.

For nine hours, through the afternoon and evening, musicians
playing rhythm and blues, soul, Cajun, zydeco, and rockabilly
entertain crowds gathered at the Prince George's Equestrian
Center. Past artists have included Delbert McClinton, Rockin
Doopsie and the Zydeco Twisters, Beausoleil, and Carl Perkins.
Food served through the day includes southern barbecue, Mary-
land seafood, and Louisiana dishes like crawdads, red beans and
rice, boudin, and Cajun sausage. The Prince George's Equestrian
Center is the site of the 1700s Marlboro Thoroughbred Race
Track, and George Washington raced there with the Alexandria
Hunt Club.

Admission: $18; $11 in advance.
Location: Prince George's Equestrian Center.
Information: Prince George's Equestrian Center, (301) 952-4740.
Tourist Information: Prince George's County Conference and
Visitors Bureau, (301) 967-8687.

Artscape

Baltimore, Md., second or third weekend in July.

Baltimore's annual salute to the arts has featured such headliners as Emmylou Harris, Ray Charles, Roberta Flack, Wynton
Marsalis, Joan Baez, Martha Reeves, Sarah Vaughn, Leon Red-
bone, and Jeffrey Osborne. The festival has also included the
Baltimore Clarinet Quartet, the Old World Folk Band, Trinidad
steel drum player Othello Molineaux, banjo star Bela Fleck and
the Flecktones, Creole music band Buckwheat Zydeco, and jazz
pianist Ahmad Jamal. If that's not enough, there are poetry

readings, literary readings, contemporary dance, film, vaudeville, comedy, street theater, and children's performances.

Artscape generally runs Friday evening and Saturday and Sunday afternoons and evenings, and is held in the Mount Royal Cultural District, home of the Joseph Meyerhoff Symphony Hall, the Lyric Opera House, and the Maryland Institute, College of Art. While musicians perform on the two outdoor stages, a number of arts exhibitions are on view at the Maryland Institute, College of Art. Children can enjoy crafts workshops, storytelling, and puppet shows at various locations. And several dozen vendors on Mount Royal Avenue offer a sampling of some of Baltimore's finest restaurants.

Admission: free.
Location: Mount Royal Cultural District.
Information: The Mayor's Advisory Committee on Art and Culture, (410) 396-4575.
Tourist Information: Baltimore Area Convention and Visitors Association, (410) 659-7300.

Latin American Festival
Washington, D.C., fourth weekend in July.

Washington's annual Hispanic festival, first held in 1970, begins its second and most active day on Sunday with the city's most colorful parade. For more than three hours, Mexican mariachi bands, elaborately costumed revelers, floats representing each Latin American country, and scores of dancers pass before onlookers lining Constitution Avenue.

The parade ends at the Washington Monument, where a crowd of 100,000 gathers for an afternoon of Latino food and entertainment. More than a hundred vendors sell the native dishes of Mexico, Bolivia, Peru, Nicaragua, and other Latin American countries. At several stages the crowd is treated to musical performances, which have included popular performers from Latin American countries and such well-known American musicians as Ruben Blades.

A minifestival is usually held Saturday in Washington's Adams

Carnival reveler at the Latin American Festival.

Morgan neighborhood, where the Latin American Festival originated. In the afternoon, local groups perform on stage and several dozen booths sell Latin American food and handmade crafts. Other events associated with the festival include a beauty pageant, a gala at a Washington hotel, and crowning of the festival queen.

Admission: free.

Location: Adams Morgan neighborhood and the Washington Monument grounds.

Information: Washington, D.C., Convention and Visitors Association, (202) 789-7000.

New Jersey

Red, White, and Blueberry Festival
Hammonton, N.J., Sunday near July 4.

Hammonton, the "blueberry capital of the world," celebrates its
number-one crop and Independence Day with a small one-day
festival. Community groups serve blueberry pies, cakes, soda, and
ice cream, and the Ethnic Food Courtyard serves dishes of the
area's ethnic groups. Past festivals have featured performances
by such groups as the Pitman Hobo Band and Jay Walker and the
Pedestrians. The festival also includes a large antique car show,
arts and crafts, a blueberry-pie-eating contest, and children's
entertainment.

Admission: free.
Location: Hammonton Middle School grounds.
Information: Greater Hammonton Chamber of Commerce, (609)
    561-9080.

Whitesbog Blueberry Festival
Browns Mills, N.J., second Saturday in July.

At the turn of the century, Whitesbog Village was a flourishing
agricultural settlement devoted to the cultivation of cranberries
and blueberries. Today it is state property being restored as a
historic village; this blueberry festival is an annual fundraiser for
the effort. Besides providing a look at the village, the festival
offers a day of Pine Barrens entertainment, contests, and all sorts
of blueberry foods. It includes a 10-kilometer run, a two-mile fun
run, bluegrass and folk music through the afternoon, blueberry
pie eating contests for the kids, and Pine Barrens crafts.

Admission: carload, $10.
Location: Whitesbog Village, intersection of routes 70 and 530.
Information: Whitesbog Preservation Trust, (609) 893-4646.
Tourist Information: Burlington County Cultural and Heritage
    Commission, (609) 265-5958.

New Jersey Festival of Balloning

Readington, N.J., third weekend in July.

Nearly 100 colorful hot-air balloons fill the sky each evening at the New Jersey Festival of Ballooning. Almost 80,000 people attend the event to watch the balloon race and to enjoy the food and entertainment on the ground. On Saturday and Sunday afternoons visitors enjoy a 1940s USO show, an international food fair, and daredevil air shows. Other attractions include an antique car exhibit, an arts and crafts show, parachute jumps, and a revolutionary war encampment.

The evening balloon races follow a "hare and hound" format. The hare, or lead balloon, takes off, choosing its own course and altitude. Ten minutes later the other balloons—the hounds—take off, chasing after the hare. After about 30 minutes the hare pilot lands, laying out on the ground a huge X. The goal of the hounds is to drop bean bags on the X; the one hitting closest is the winner.

Balloon lift-off at the New Jersey Festival of Ballooning.

Procession through Hoboken's streets during St. Ann's Italian Festival.

Admission: adults, $10; children under 10, free.
Location: Solberg Airport, south of Somerville on U.S. Route 202.
Information: New Jersey Festival of Ballooning, Inc., (908) 236-6733.
Tourist Information: Hunterdon County Chamber of Commerce, (908) 735-5955.

St. Ann's Italian Festival

Hoboken, N.J., week preceding July 26.

July 26 is the Feast of St. Ann, when the women of Hoboken's St. Ann's Roman Catholic Church carry a 600-pound statue of the saint through the streets of the city. The procession and festival, which dates to 1910, honors Christ's grandmother, who gave birth to the Virgin Mary at age 60. St. Ann is the patron saint of pregnant women, and the women who bear the saint are often those who wish to become pregnant.

The festival runs each evening the week before the feast day and all of the feast day itself. The church's courtyard becomes the Cafe under the Stars, with green, white, and red decorations, umbrella-covered tables, strolling entertainers, and Italian food— including the festival's famous zeppole, a sugar-covered fried dough made by St. Ann's Guild. Stage entertainment has included Connie Francis, Marty De Rose and the Dom Perry Orchestra, and the New Jersey State Opera. A special night is devoted to the music of Frank Sinatra, a Hoboken native and a visitor to the festival with Ronald Reagan in 1984.

Admission: free.

Location: St. Ann's Roman Catholic Church, Seventh and Jefferson streets.

Information: St. Ann's Roman Catholic Church, (201) 659-1114.

Tourist Information: Hudson County Chamber of Commerce, (201) 653-7400.

New York

Friendship Festival

Buffalo, N.Y., first week in July.

Celebrating friendship between the United States and Canada, the Friendship Festival is held in Buffalo and in Fort Erie, Ontario, during the week when both nations celebrate their birthdays. There are a variety of activities, including evening performances that have featured such top names as Natalie Cole, Conway Twitty, and the Commodores. One popular event, usually held on Saturday, is Kidspace, with big-top entertainment, face painting, kite building, clown and juggling workshops, games, and races. Another highlight is the International Airshow, which features aircraft stunts, military displays, and wingwalking over the Niagara River. Other activities have included Highland games, horse shows, an arts and crafts show, balloon races, and stunt-kite demonstrations.

Admission: most activities are free.

Location: LaSalle Park in Buffalo, and Niagara Parkway and
   Mather Arch in Fort Erie, Ontario.
Information: Greater Buffalo Chamber of Commerce, (716) 852-
   2761.
Tourist Information: Greater Buffalo Convention and Visitors
   Bureau, (800) 283-3256 or (716) 852-0511.

Feast of Our Lady of Mt. Carmel and St. Paulinus of Nola

Brooklyn, N.Y., 12 days ending on July 16.

The giglio, an 85-foot-tall, three-ton tower holding an orchestra
and topped with a statue of St. Paulinus, is carried on the shoul-
ders of 120 men down North Eighth Street in Brooklyn. During
the dance of the giglio (pronounced jeel-yo), the men carrying the
giglio sometimes do the cha-cha, sometimes fancy dance steps like
the "number two," a quick drop and lift of the giglio, or the "three-
sixty," where they spin the giglio completely around. Another
group of men carry a boat loaded with sailors and a smaller
orchestra.

The pageant honors St. Paulinus, who was bishop of Nola,
Italy, in the fifth century. Legend holds that Bishop Paulinus
offered himself in place of a widow's only son when Spanish
conquerors took captured villagers to North Africa. But the bishop
impressed his captors with his gift of prophecy and soon won the
release of all. When they returned to Nola, the villagers greeted
them with many bouquets of lilies, and the huge pile of flowers
inspired the first giglio, whose name is Italian for lily. For hundreds of years Nola has celebrated the Feast of St. Paulinus, now
with eight giglios. When Nola emigrants settled in Brooklyn in
the late nineteenth century, they continued the feast-day celebration, which is now more than a hundred years old.

The Feast of Our Lady of Mt. Carmel runs for 12 days, up to
and including July 16, the Feast of St. Paulinus. Each evening on
North Eighth and Havemeyer streets, vendors sell sausages,
zepolles, and other Italian food, and entertainment is scheduled
on the church steps. The dance of the giglio runs each Sunday
afternoon.

Admission: free.
Location: North Eighth and Havemeyer streets, Williamsburg section of Brooklyn.
Information: Church of Our Lady of Mt. Carmel, (718) 384-0223.
Tourist Information: New York Convention and Visitors Bureau, (212) 397-8222.

German Alps Festival

Hunter, N.Y., first three weeks in July (closed Mondays).

Hunter Mountain in the northern Catskills becomes a German village in July, with men wearing lederhosen, oompah bands, folk dancers, and German food and beer. Of the 150 performers, nearly half come from Germany, such as the Stadtkapelle Kempten, a 35-piece brass band, and Almrausch Schuhplattlers, a Bavarian folk-dance group. Past festivals have also included strolling musicians, accordion players, a falconer, and the Clydesdale horses. A highlight of the festival is the M. I. Hummelfest, which showcases Hummel figurines, steins, and crystal and Goebel dolls. The German Alps Festival runs for more than two weeks, with activities through the afternoon and evening.

Admission: adults, $8; children 12 and under, $2.
Location: Hunter Mountain.
Directions: from Catskill, New York, follow Route 23A west for 21 miles.
Information: Hunter Mountain Festivals, Ltd., (518) 263-3800.
Tourist Information: Greene County Promotion Department, (800) 542-2414 or (518) 943-3223.

Genesee Street Festival

Utica, N.Y., five days beginning Monday after July 4.

As the centerpiece of A Good Old Summer Time, Utica's summer events program, the Genesee Street Festival offers five days of stage performances, strolling musicians, wine tasting, waiters' races, ethnic singing groups, mime circuses, and rows of food vendors. Musical performances, scheduled through the afternoon and evening each day, have included ragtime bands, barbershop quartets, Elvis impersonators, bluegrass bands, and folk singers. Each day has a theme; International Day has featured bagpipe bands, Korean martial arts demonstrations, an Italian folk dancing group, and African drummers. Other activities associated with A Good Old Summer Time include the 15-kilometer Utica Boilermaker Road Race, the Erie Canal Canoe Classic, a Miss Greater Utica Pageant, and an arts and crafts show.

Admission: free.

Location: Genesee Street.

Information: A Good Old Summer Time, Inc., (315) 733-6976.

Tourist Information: Oneida County Convention and Visitors Bureau, (800) 426-3132 or (315) 724-7221.

Panama Rocks Folk Fair

Panama, N.Y., three days starting second Friday in July.

Panama Rocks is an extensive formation of quartz conglomerate cut and shaped by the continental glaciers. On a weekend in July the Panama Rocks Scenic Park holds its Folk Fair with exhibits, demonstrations, and performances. More than a hundred craftspeople sell Early American work such as china painting, dried flowers and herbs, dulcimers and 50 other traditional instruments, tole and decorative painting, Adirondack bentwood furniture, wickerware, and quilts. There are demonstrations of blacksmithing, log hewing, sheep shearing, spinning and dyeing wool, and maple-syrup making. Several hundred people appear in period costume, and there are often special exhibitions like antique quilt collections or a recreated mountainman's camp. Two bluegrass bands play back-to-back through each day at the park-green stage, and vendors sell chicken barbecue dinners, roast beef sandwiches, and other food.

Admission: adults, $4; senior citizens, $3; children ages 5–12, $2.

Location: Panama Rocks Scenic Park.

Directions: from Jamestown, New York, follow Route 394 west

Napoleon rides in the French Festival parade in Cape Vincent, New York.

7 miles; turn left on and follow Route 474 6 miles to Panama; .25 mile west of light, turn left on Rock Hill Road.

Information: Panama Rocks Folk Fair, (716) 782-2845.

Tourist Information: Chautauqua County Vacationlands, (800) 242-4569 or (716) 753-4304.

French Festival

Cape Vincent, N.Y., second Saturday in July.

The village of Cape Vincent, on the St. Lawrence River, was settled by the French around 1800; followers of Napoleon once planned to bring him there in exile. Today the people of Cape Vincent celebrate their heritage with a French Festival. The day-long event begins on the main street of the village, where vendors push decorated French carts selling French pastry, bread, and ice cream, as well as berets, balloons, and flags. Opening ceremonies late in the morning include the crowning of the French Festival Queen. Later, in the afternoon, Cape Vincent's own Napoleon on horseback leads a parade through the village streets, followed by marching-band performances at the reviewing stand. In the evening, a French Mass is held at the St. Vincent de Paul Church. Through the afternoon and evening, the Lake and River Parish United Church holds a French buffet dinner. The festival ends with a fireworks display at the waterfront.

Admission: free.
Location: throughout the village.
Information: Cape Vincent Chamber of Commerce, (315) 654-2481.
Directions: from Watertown, follow Route 12E to Cape Vincent.
Tourist Information: 1000 Islands International Council, (800) 847-5263 or (315) 482-2520.

Corn Hill Arts Festival

Rochester, N.Y., weekend after July 4.

It is believed Corn Hill got its name because the area was once planted in corn, and boat captains on the Genesee River knew they had reached Rochester when they saw the "Corn Hill." In the early nineteenth century Rochester's wealthiest residents built homes there, and the neighborhood knew such notables as Susan B. Anthony, Harriet Tubman, and Ralph Avery. Today Corn Hill is a revitalized landmark community, with tree-lined streets, restored Victorian homes, and carefully designed twentieth-century townhouses and condominiums.

The neighborhood's strong community spirit is most evident during the Corn Hill Arts Festival. Some 450 artists from across the United States, Canada, and Europe exhibit their work and compete in a variety of categories. The show ranges from conventional items like drawings, sculpture, and pottery to bonsai trees and handcrafted musical instruments. There is also a wide variety of music, including blues singers, oompah bands, Dixieland jazz bands, and Celtic folk singers. Food is diverse as well, with samplings of Italian, Chinese, Caribbean, and Polish specialties. The festival also offers street performers, a rugby tournament, and rescue demonstrations.

Admission: free.

Location: Corn Hill neighborhood, Exchange Boulevard and Atkinson Street.

Information: Greater Rochester Visitors Association, (716) 546-3070.

Taste of Buffalo

Buffalo, N.Y., weekend after July 4.

Lined up along Main Street, Buffalo's most interesting restaurants offer their favorite dishes, all priced between 50 cents and $2.50. Curly's Bar and Grill serves its Jamaican jerk chicken and warm pork salad; Joe's Broadway Market, pierogi and duck soup; Gramma Mora's, apple grande and Mexican sundaes; Santasieros, pasta fazzulla and lentils and macaroni; Yip Lee Chinese Restaurant, beef teriyaki and chicken lo mein; Colter Bay Grill, barbi shrimp on a skewer and Cotton Creek salad; and Melanie's Sweets Unlimited, custard ice cream cones and cannoli. Meanwhile, on three stages spread along Buffalo Place, musicians perform swing, classic rock and roll, Carribean music, soul, rhythm and blues, show tunes, Italian folk tunes, German oompah music, and Dixieland jazz. A children's stage features magic shows and storytelling, and a Karaoke stage gives audience members a chance to stand on stage and sing their favorite tune. The festival benefits a food-related charity, such as Meals On Wheels. It runs Saturday and Sunday from late morning through the evening.

Admission: free.

Location: Buffalo Place, Main Street.

Information: Taste of Buffalo, Inc., (716) 834-9108.

Tourist Information: Greater Buffalo Convention and Visitors Bureau, (800) 283-3256 or (716) 852-0511.

Tupper Lake Woodsmen's Days

Tupper Lake, N.Y., second weekend in July.

Sitting in the center of the Adirondack Mountains, Tupper Lake celebrates the local logging industry with a festival in July. The weekend event includes many competitions, such as chain sawing, woodchopping, log rolling, and buck sawing. The horse-pulling contest tests workhorse teams' ability to pull heavy weights. At the Northeastern Chainsaw Carving Competition, artists create sculptures with a log and a chainsaw. The festival runs all day Saturday and Sunday afternoon.

Admission: $3; children under 10, free.
Location: Municipal Park.
Information: Tupper Lake Woodsmen's Association, (518) 359-9444.
Tourist Information: Tupper Lake Chamber of Commerce, (518) 359-3328.

Can-Am Festival

Sackets Harbor, N.Y., third weekend in July.

During the War of 1812, Sackets Harbor on Lake Ontario was the nation's most important shipbuilding center, with a third of the U.S. Army and a quarter of the Navy stationed there. Today, on a weekend in late July, the quaint village celebrates the two battles fought there and the peace with Canada that has existed since.

The Can-Am Festival features land and sea battle reenactments on Saturday afternoon, and tactical demonstrations are usually held at Market Square Park on Sunday. The festival also includes a Miss Can-Am Pageant, Friday and Saturday evening dances, polo matches, children's entertainment, a two-day crafts fair, a parade Saturday morning, and a chicken barbecue along with other food.

Admission: free.

Location: throughout the village and at Sackets Harbor Battlefield.
Information: Can-Am Festival, (315) 646-2321.
Tourist Information: 1000 Islands International Council, (800) 847-5263 or (315) 482-2520.

Ukrainian Youth Festival

Glen Spey, N.Y., third weekend in July.

Verkhovyna, the Ukrainian resort in the Catskills, offers a weekend festival of Ukrainian dance, music, crafts, and food. Programs, scheduled Friday evening, Saturday afternoon and evening, and Sunday afternoon, feature the Verkhovyna Dance Workshop, performing folk dances and ballet. There are also performances by musical ensembles, choirs, and dance groups from the Ukraine. After the performances Friday and Saturday evening, orchestras play Ukrainian, rock, and other music, and dancing lasts into the night. Some 70 exhibitors show and sell Ukrainian embroidery, handmade jewelry, Trypillian and Hutzul ceramics, icons, and other crafts. Vendors on the resort's grounds sell stuffed cabbage, pierogi, and fried chicken, and the main dining room serves cossack dinners of wurst, stuffed cabbage, and sauerkraut.

Admission: free.
Location: Ukrainian Fraternal Association Resort Center Verkhovyna.
Directions: from Port Jervis, New York, follow N.Y. Route 97 for 10 miles to Pond Eddy; turn right and follow County Route 41 for 1 mile.
Information: Ukrainian Fraternal Association, (717) 342-0937.
Tourist Information: Sullivan County Office of Public Information, (800) 882-2287 or (914) 794-3000 ext. 5010.

Winterhawk Bluegrass Festival

Hillsdale, N.Y., third weekend in July.

Winterhawk Bluegrass Festival is one of the top bluegrass festivals in the Northeast. Bill Monroe, Ralph Stanley, Frank

Wakefield, the Lewis Family, Peter Rowan, the Del McCoury
Band, and Doc Watson are some of the well-known bluegrass
performers who have appeared. The festival begins Thursday
evening, with all-day performances Friday, Saturday, and Sunday. Many of those attending buy four-day tickets and camp at
the festival site. The festival also offers workshops, teen dances,
a talent search, a band competition, and a full range of food
concessions.

Admission: various early-bird, weekend, and day tickets.
Location: Rothvoss Farm, 8 miles south of Hillsdale on Route 22.
Information: Winterhawk, (513) 390-6211.
Tourist Information: Columbia County Planning and Economic
    Development Department, (800) 777-9247 or (518) 828-3375.

The Main Event

Rochester, N.Y., weekend in late July.

The Main Event is Rochester's downtown summer street festival,
a weekend of music, food, and sports. Held on a mile-long section
of Main Street, the festival begins Friday evening with a celebrity
basketball game; Governor Mario Cuomo sometimes joins the fun.
Throughout Saturday and Sunday, five stages provide a variety
of entertainment, from ethnic dancing and classic rock to
storytelling and jazz. The festival also includes craft demonstrations, street dances, an art show, and a Saturday night fireworks
show.

Admission: free.
Location: Main Street.
Information: Greater Rochester Visitors Association, Inc., (716)
    546-3070.

Canal Fest

*Tonawanda and North Tonawanda, N.Y., last full week in
July.*

The Erie Canal gave birth to the twin cities of Tonawanda and

North Tonawanda, and today the communities celebrate the canal with a week-long festival. Held on the banks of the canal and at locations throughout both towns, the event offers hydroplane races on the Niagara River, marionette shows, boat parades, water skiing shows, carnival rides, children's activities, and musical performances. Entertainment has included local choruses, Dixieland bands, barbershop quartets, square dancers, banjo bands, and classic rock groups. Churches and community groups sell chowder, goulash dinners, and baked goods.

Admission: free.

Location: banks of Erie Barge Canal and various other locations in Tonawanda and North Tonawanda.

Information: Chamber of Commerce of the Tonawandas, (716) 692-5120.

Harborfest
Oswego, N.Y., last weekend in July.

Oswego was the first American harbor on the Great Lakes. Each July the town celebrates its heritage with more than 100 musical performances, arts and crafts, fine arts, antiques, a Civil War encampment, an antique and classic boat show, and a catch-all bazaar. Three stages are in full swing throughout the festival, during the afternoon and evening on Friday and Saturday and on Sunday afternoon. Headliner evening concerts held at the Main Stage have featured Don McLean, the Drifters, and Wild Rose. One of the biggest draws is the Saturday night Grucci fireworks show, which is choreographed to music. The festival runs Thursday evening through Sunday evening and also includes a children's park with magicians, mimes, storytelling, and a children's parade. Tall ships give a display, and there are sailboat races and water-rescue demonstrations.

Admission: free.

Location: throughout the city.

Information: Harbor Festivals, Inc., (315) 343-6858.

Tourist Information: Oswego County Tourism Department, (800) 248-4386 or (315) 349-8322.

Fireworks over Oswego's harbor during Harborfest.

Onondaga Lake Waterfront Extravaganza
Liverpool, N.Y., last weekend in July.

Celebrating Onondaga Lake, the Waterfront Extravaganza features evening concerts by well-known groups such as Beatlemania, the Platters, and the Tommy Dorsey Orchestra. Each afternoon and evening Thursday through Sunday, entertainment is scheduled at four locations. The festival has included a Wild West Show, Freihofer's Mime Circus and Juggling Jamboree, and the Water Circus, a group of stunt water-skiers who perform jumps, triple pyramids, and high-speed water acrobatics. There are also food, boat cruises, arts and crafts, and a fireworks show on the lake.

Admission: free.
Location: Onondaga Lake Park.
Information: Onondaga County Parks, (315) 451-7275.

Tourist Information: Syracuse-Onondaga Convention and Visitors Bureau, (800) 234-4797 or (315) 470-1800.

New York Renaissance Festival

Tuxedo Park, N.Y., weekends from last weekend in July to third weekend in September.

Each weekend Sterling Forest becomes a sixteenth-century English country fair with a recreated Tudor village, hundreds of authentically costumed entertainers, craftspeople demonstrating and selling their work, and food and drink. Professional acting troupes perform Shakespeare's plays and other works on five stages. Strolling musicians, jesters, and village characters mingle with the crowds. Knights in shining armor joust in the meadow. Craftspeople demonstrate glassblowing, chain-mail linking, and blacksmithing. Village pubs serve turkey drumsticks, steak-on-a-stake, stuffed spuds, and meat pies. The festival runs late morning and afternoon Saturday and Sunday.

Admission: adults, $12.75; children ages 6–12, $5; senior citizens, $10.75; advance sales and group rates available.
Location: Sterling Forest, N.Y. Route 17A.
Information: New York Renaissance Festival, (914) 351-5171.
Tourist Information: Hudson River Valley Association, (800) 232-4782 or (914) 229-0033.

Pennsylvania

Pennsylvania Renaissance Faire

Manheim, Pa., last weekend in June through second weekend in October.

See June—Pennsylvania.

RiverBlues Festival

Philadelphia, Pa., weekend sometime in July.

At RiverBlues some of the nation's top blues artists perform a varied range of blues styles, from the down-home country blues of the Mississippi Delta to the hard-driving, party-time blues of Chicago honky-tonks. Considered one of the best blues festivals on the East Coast, RiverBlues features more than 20 bands performing on four riverfront stages. Past entertainers have included B. B. King, Johnny Winter, Albert Collins, Elvin Bishop, and James Cotton. Food served includes Philadelphia cheese steaks and hoagies, barbecued chicken, and batter-dipped veggies. The festival runs through the afternoon and evening Saturday and Sunday.

Admission: adults, $14, in advance, $10; children ages 2–12, $1.
Location: Penn's Landing.
Information: RiverBlues Festival, (215) 636-1666.
Tourist Information: Philadelphia Convention and Visitors Bureau, (800) 321-9563 or (215) 636-1666.

Kutztown Folk Festival

Kutztown, Pa., Independence Day week.

The Kutztown Folk Festival is a glimpse into the Pennsylvania Dutch culture, where more than 200 craftspeople create eighteenth- and nineteenth-century handmade items. There are demonstrations of candle dipping, pottery making, sheep shearing, and blacksmithing. The Amish do not participate in the festival because of their religious beliefs, but actors reenact an Amish wedding. Another popular attraction is the Quilting Building, where 1,700 quilts are displayed.

The Kutztown Folk Festival is one of Pennsylvania's most popular festivals, attracting more than 100,000 people. It runs for nine days, morning through early evening each day. At the three main stages there are performances of Pennsylvania Dutch music, hoedowning and jigging demonstrations, and a country auc-

Quilt making at the Kutztown Folk Festival.

tion. Demonstrations of Pennsylvania Dutch crafts and culture are also scheduled each day. Food includes such Pennsylvania Dutch treats as stuffed noodles, chow-chow, and shoofly pie.

Admission: adults, $7; children, $3.
Location: Kutztown Fairgrounds.
Information: Pennsylvania Folklife Society, (215) 683-8707.
Tourist Information: Berks County Visitors Information
    Association, (800) 443-6610 or (215) 375-4085.

Bark Peelers' Convention

Galeton, Pa., weekend closest to July 4.

The Pennsylvania Lumber Museum preserves and exhibits the colorful logging history of north-central Pennsylvania, and the Bark Peelers' Convention brings that history to life with two days of lumberjack contests. In the greased pole contest, two contestants mount a horizontal greased pole and attempt to knock the other off with a pillow. The tobacco-spitting contest tests contestants' skill at hitting a hot potbellied stove from seven feet. The birling contest requires contestants to stay on a white-pine log in the museum's pond. The festival also has a fiddler's competition, a frog jumping contest for the kids, crafts, and musical entertainment.

Admission: adults, $4; children, $2.
Location: Pennsylvania Lumber Museum, U.S. Route 6.
Directions: from Galeton follow U.S. Route 6 west for 10 miles.
Information: Pennsylvania Lumber Museum, (814) 435-2652.
Tourist Information: Potter County Recreation, Inc., (814) 435-2290.

Philadelphia Freedom Festival

Philadelphia, Pa., July 4 to following Sunday.

The Declaration of Independence was signed in Philadelphia on July 4, 1776, so it is only natural for the city to sponsor an outstanding Fourth of July festival. For example, after the usual patriotic ceremonies in the morning, an 80-foot by 10-foot birthday cake is cut and served to more than 10,000 people, and all join government officials and celebrities in singing "Happy Birthday." At Penn's Landing, on the city's waterfront, a Restaurant Festival runs for several days, offering the specialties of 20 Philadelphia eateries plus entertainment. The Great American Balloon Race, taking off from Von Colln Field and the Benjamin Franklin Parkway, celebrates the first hot-air balloon launch from Walnut Street in Philadelphia on January 19, 1793. The length and schedule of events of the Philadelphia Freedom Festival varies from year to year, but the event usually offers musical performances ranging from pop to patriotic, an Independence Day Parade, and a fireworks extravaganza.

Admission: free.
Location: Independence National Park and other locations in Philadelphia.

Information: Office of the City Representative, (215) 686-2876.
Tourist Information: Philadelphia Convention and Visitors
Bureau, (800) 321-9563 or (215) 636-1666.

Central Pennsylvania Festival of the Arts
State College, Pa., week after July 4.

During the second week of July, State College's downtown streets
and part of the Penn State campus become a festive bazaar, with
hundreds of artists selling paintings, photography, sculpture,
handwoven clothing, pottery, jewelry, and woodwork. More than
a thousand artists apply for the event, which attracts 250,000
visitors over five days, but less than 400 artists qualify to show
and sell their work.

Begun in 1967, when a handful of local artists exhibited their
work on a wall, the arts festival is now Central Pennsylvania's
biggest summertime event. It begins on Wednesday—a day before
the artists show up—with Children's Day, offering clowns, face
painting, and storytelling.

Through the rest of the week, when the crowds arrive, local
and national entertainers perform at four stages scattered about
town. One of the highlights of the festival is the variety of music,
which ranges from classical to reggae to bluegrass. Other activities include a hot-air balloon race and a film series.

Admission: free.
Location: downtown State College and campus of Pennsylvania
State University.
Information: Central Pennsylvania Festival of the Arts, (814)
237-3682.
Tourist Information: Centre County Lion Country Visitors and
Convention Bureau, (800) 358-5466 or (814) 231-1400.

Canal Festival
Easton, Pa., first or second Saturday in July.

Celebrating the history of canal boating, Easton's Canal Festival is held in Hugh Moore Historical Park on the restored Lehigh Canal. One of the three entertainment stages is aboard the *Josiah White*, a mule-drawn canal boat that gives rides along the canal. A highlight of the one-day event is the Canal Boatmen's Reunion, which includes men who worked on the Lehigh Canal and the nearby Delaware Canal before they closed in 1932. The boatmen share tales of the bygone towpath canal days with festivalgoers. The Canal Festival runs Saturday morning and afternoon. Musical performances run continuously and include folk, polka, ragtime, and Dixieland. At a small crafts show, 75 regional artists demonstrate, exhibit, and sell their work. There is also a children's area and food concessions.

Admission: $3 per car.

Location: Hugh Moore Historical Park.

Information: Hugh Moore Historical Park and Museums, (215) 250-6700.

Tourist Information: Lehigh Valley Convention and Visitors Bureau, Inc., (800) 747-0561 or (215) 266-0560.

Somerfest

Somerset, Pa., second or third weekend in July.

Somerset's summer celebration of the arts features a juried art show, an arts and crafts market with artist demonstrations, continuous live entertainment, and children's activities like face painting, storytelling, and crafts. Performances include folk, jazz, big-band, barbershop, and contemporary rock music. Among the old favorites are the Fiddlin' Fisher Family, the Coal Country Cloggers, and the Steel City Stompers Zany Comedy Band. The festival officially kicks off Friday night with a parade and continues through the afternoon and evening on Saturday and Sunday.

Admission: adults, $3; senior citizens, $2; children 12 and under, free.

Location: Philip Dressler Center for the Arts, Harrison Avenue.

Information: Laurel Arts, Inc., (814) 443-2433 or 443-1835.

Tourist Information: Laurel Highlands, Inc., (800) 333-5661 or (412) 238-5661.

New Growth Arts Festival

Indiana, Pa., third weekend in July.

Named for the new growth of Indiana County's famous Christ-mas tree crop, the New Growth Arts Festival offers entertain-ment on three stages, with mostly western Pennsylvania musi-cians performing jazz, big band, bluegrass, top 40s, ethnic, oldies, and folk. Mimes, jugglers, and puppeteers also appear; a Children's Alley features a wide variety of hands-on activities for children. The weekend event attracts 60 artists, who participate in a juried show with three different exhibitions. Other activities include dance demonstrations, a five-kilometer run, and a Friday evening ox roast.

Admission: free.
Location: Philadelphia Street in downtown Indiana.
Information: New Growth Arts Festival, (412) 357-2787.
Tourist Information: Indiana County Visitors and Convention Bureau, (412) 463-7505.

Chambersfest

Chambersburg, Pa., last week of July.

When Confederate troops captured Chambersburg, Pennsylva-nia, in 1864, they demanded a ransom of $500,000 in U.S. cur-rency or $100,000 in gold. The residents refused, and the Confed-erates burned the town, destroying more than 500 buildings. Rebuilding began almost immediately, and within several years the town's streets were lined with some of the finest architecture of the time. Today, Chambersburg celebrates the burning and the town's rebirth with an annual festival.

Chambersfest runs for about a week. Most activities are sched-uled for the weekend and include Celebrate! The Arts, with vocal and organ recitals, bands, children's theater, and arts and crafts exhibits. Among other events are Civil War seminars, an air show, evening concerts, living history performances, and historic tours.

Admission: free; charges for some events.
Location: downtown.
Information: Chambersburg Chamber of Commerce, (717) 264-7101.
Tourist Information: Cumberland Valley Visitors' Council, (717) 261-1200.

Scenic River Days

Reading, Pa., last week in July.

Scenic River Days, Reading's biggest summer event, is a celebration of music, art, food, and fun. Continuous performances are scheduled at four stages, and a Main Tent features concerts by top-name performers. These have included Dizzy Gillespie, Maria Muldaur, the Smothers Brothers, Spyro Gyra, the Woody Herman Orchestra, Bobby Vinton, B. B. King, and Tammy Wynette. A wide range of music is scheduled, such as Celtic, rhythm and

Children's entertainer at Reading's Scenic River Days.

blues, swing, Latin jazz, polka, a cappella, reggae, and country and western. The festival also offers kids' programs, a juried art show, exhibits, a bike race, and foods, including Pennsylvania Dutch dishes like pork and sauerkraut, chicken potpie, apple dumplings, and shoofly pie.

Admission: free; charge for Main Tent performances.
Location: River Front Park.
Information: Berks Festivals, (215) 375-6508.
Tourist Information: Berks County Visitors Information Association, (800) 443-6610 or (215) 375-4085.

Bavarian Fun Fest

Sharon, Pa., last weekend in July, first weekend in August.

Sharon's Bavarian Fun Fest is one of western Pennsylvania's largest festivals, with two long weekends of European music, dance, crafts, and food. Under giant beer-hall tents, three stages feature more than 1,600 performers, including oompah bands, polka bands, tamburitza players, large *blaskapelle* orchestras, marching bagpipers, German folk dancers, Italian singers, bluegrass bands, rock-and-roll groups, and military concert bands. Two large dance floors are filled with dancers throughout both weekends.

The festival runs Thursday and Friday evening and Saturday and Sunday afternoon and evening for two weekends. There is a theme for each day, including a number of ethnic celebrations with special food and entertainment: Slovene Day, International Day, Italian Day, and Polish Day. The festival offers a wide variety of food, such as German wurst, open-pit beef, barbecued chicken, Bavarian strudel, and an assortment of beers. The festival also includes children's entertainment, artisans' demonstrations, strolling entertainers, and a firefighter's parade.

Admission: adults, $4.50; senior citizens and children ages 10–13 with adult, $2.50; children under 10, free with adult; early-bird and special rates.
Location: Old Express Restaurant complex in downtown.

Information: Old Express Restaurant, (412) 981-3123.
Tourist Information: Mercer County Tourist Promotion Office,
(412) 981-5880.

Rain Day Festival

Waynesburg, Pa., July 29.

More than a hundred years ago a farmer remarked to Waynesburg's
pharmacist that it always seemed to rain on July 29. The pharmacist, a meticulous record-keeper, then began jotting down in
his daybook whether it had rained on that day, and his records
soon confirmed that it nearly always did rain on July 29. The
pharmacist's brother continued the record-keeping and began a
yearly all-night vigil in which the townsmen would sit around a
keg of beer and wait for the first raindrops. In the 1920s the new
owner of the drugstore took over the record-keeping and began
the tradition of betting traveling salesmen their hat that it would
rain on July 29.

Rain has fallen on July 29 in Waynesburg, Pennsylvania, 97
out of 114 years. Today the town celebrates with a day-long
festival that includes an umbrella decorating contest, turtle and
toad races, food and craft booths, and entertainment at the Court
House. Past years have featured musical groups such as
Beatlemania, the Platters, and the Vogues. The town now bets
celebrities and has won hats from Willard Scott, Bob Hope, and
Johnny Carson.

Admission: free.
Location: Main Street.
Information: Waynesburg Borough Offices, (412) 627-8111.
Tourist Information: Laurel Highlands, Inc., (800) 333-5661 or
(412) 238-5661.

Virginia

Festival of Nations

Norfolk, Va., weekend in July or August.

Norfolk's Festival of Nations begins with a mass naturalization ceremony performed by a federal judge and accompanied by music of the U.S. Atlantic Fleet Band. Then, for the rest of the weekend, festivalgoers are taken on a trip around the world through the music, dance, and food of more than a dozen nations. Stage entertainment has featured the Caribbean Steel Drum Band, the Filipino Folk Dancers, Meiki's Tamure Polynesian Revue, and the Italian Quartet. Ethnic groups serve a wide variety of foods, such as enjera-dorowatt (spiced chicken and egg on soft bread) from Ethiopia, lahipurakka (salmon pie) from Finland, heitar pylsur (Icelandic-style hot dog), tabouli salad from Lebanon, and tortillas d'bacalado (catfish tortilla) from Spain. There also are workshops, demonstrations, and a children's area with international games, hands-on crafts, and a puppet theater.

Admission: free.
Location: Town Point Park.
Information: Festevents, Ltd., (804) 627-7809.
Tourist Information: Norfolk Convention and Visitors Bureau, (804) 441-5266.

Clarksville Lakefest

Clarksville, Va., third weekend in July.

Clarksville sits on Buggs Island Lake, the largest lake in Virginia. In July the town celebrates life on the lake with three days of music, food, and special activities. Besides country singers and bluegrass bands, the festival offers a Beach Music Festival, sponsored by the local fire company. Local groups also serve up good food: the local rescue squad hosts a Pig Pickin' Feast and the Jaycees hold a fish fry at Occoneechee Park. The festival also includes an arts and crafts show, a giant flea market, paratrooper demonstrations, hot-air balloons, magic shows, and karate and gymnastic demonstrations.

Admission: free.
Location: Occoneechee State Park and Virginia Avenue, Clarksville.
Information: Clarksville Chamber of Commerce, (804) 374-2436.

Pork, Peanut, and Pine Festival
Surry, Va., third weekend in July.

In late July, Surry County celebrates its major products, two of which are good to eat. Barbecue sandwiches, chitterlings, ham biscuits, crackling, pigs' feet, grilled pork chops, and pit-cooked barbecue are among the pork dishes churches and community groups sell at the festival. Peanuts are served plain or in dishes like peanut-raisin pie, peanut cookies, peanut soup, peanut brittle, and spiced and sugared peanuts. The festival's two stages provide continuous gospel, country, and jazz music, and local craftspeople display and sell quilts, pottery, glass, and other work. There are also exhibits for the third industry—loblolly pine harvesting for lumber and paper. The festival is held at Chippokes Plantation State Park, an eighteenth-century farm where Virginia farm life of the past three centuries is re-created.

Admission: parking, $2.
Location: Chippokes Plantation State Park.
Directions: from Surry follow Route 10 south, then turn left on and follow Route 634 for 3 miles.
Information: Chippokes Plantation State Park, (804) 294-3625.
Tourist Information: Surry County Chamber of Commerce, (804) 294-3907.

Chincoteague Volunteer Firemen's Pony Roundup and Swim

Chincoteague Island, Va., last Wednesday and Thursday in July.

Since 1924, the volunteer firefighters of Chincoteague have rounded up the wild ponies on Assateague Island and herded them across a narrow channel to Chincoteague Island, where they are corralled and auctioned off. No one knows for sure how the ponies first arrived on Assateague Island. One legend is that ponies swam to the island from shipwrecked Spanish galleons in the 1500s. Another holds that they belonged to pirates who used the island as a hideout, but were forced to leave without the ponies. Pony roundups date back to the early settlers, who sold the animals on the mainland. The modern roundup, though, raises

Hammer throw competition at the Virginia Scottish Games.

money for the fire department and helps control the pony population in the Chincoteague National Wildlife Refuge.

More than 30,000 people come to watch the roundup and swim on Wednesday morning. The first colt across becomes King or Queen Neptune and is given away to one of those attending. The auctioning of the foals is held on Thursday, and the remaining ponies swim back to Assateague on Friday. The roundup and auction occur during the firefighter's two-week carnival. There is entertainment during the roundup and auction, and community groups serve breakfasts and dinners.

Admission: free.

Location: South Main Street and Memorial Park.

Information: Chincoteague Chamber of Commerce, (804) 336-6161.

Tourist Information: Eastern Shore Tourism Commission, (804) 787-2460.

Virginia Scottish Games
Alexandria, Va., fourth weekend in July.

The Scottish games were first held in the eleventh century, when King Malcolm of Scotland organized foot races to find the best runners for carrying messages. Over the years other events were added, all of them related to common country tasks in old Scotland. In the tossing of the sheaf, a pitchfork was used to throw a 16-pound bag of straw over a pole. A blacksmith's hammer was originally used for the hammer throw, and a round stone from the river for putting the stone. Woodsmen used tree trunks for their caber toss.

Brawny men in kilts compete in these ancient events today at the Virginia Scottish Games. The festival also features the National Scottish Fiddling Championship, the Celtic Harp Competition, Highland dancing competitions, and bagpipe band competitions. There are sheepdog demonstrations, Celtic entertainment, and Scottish food like meat pies, bridies, and shortbread. The Virginia Scottish Games generally run morning through evening on Saturday and morning and afternoon on Sunday.

Admission: one-day ticket, $9; two-day ticket, $15; children ages 15 and under free with paying adult, advance ticket rates.

Location: Episcopal High School grounds, 3901 West Braddock Road.

Directions: from King Street Exit off I-395 follow King Street east to West Braddock Road; shuttle buses run from the King Street metro station.

Information: Alexandria Convention and Visitors Bureau, (703) 838-4200.

Virginia Highlands Festival

Abingdon, Va., last weekend of July and first two weeks in August.

Daniel Boone encountered a pack of wolves at a cave in 1760 and named the spot Wolf Hill. Later, the frontier settlement changed its name to Abingdon after Martha Washington's English hometown. Today Abingdon, Virginia, preserves its heritage with restored log cabins, Federal and Victorian architecture, and brick sidewalks under sweet gums and boxwoods. For two weeks at the end of July, the quaint town celebrates its cultural heritage with the Virginia Highlands Festival.

Over 150,000 people come to the festival for musical performances, a juried arts and crafts show, historic reenactments and lectures, creative writing and art workshops, historic home tours, performances at the Barter Theatre, the Big Feast Balloon Rally, nature programs, and a gourmet food fair. One major attraction of the festival is the antique market, with 135 booths. Musical performances, held at various times and locations, include bagpipe, classical, bluegrass, folk, rock and roll, and chamber music. Special youth events feature storytelling, music, puppet shows, and a children's flea market.

Admission: free; charges for some activities.

Location: downtown Abingdon and Virginia Highlands Community College.

Information: Washington County Chamber of Commerce, (703) 628-8141.

Tourist Information: Abingdon Visitors and Convention Bureau, (703) 676-2282.

West Virginia

Mountain State Art and Craft Fair
Ripley, W.Va., Independence Day week.

Considered the "granddaddy" of West Virginia crafts festivals, the Mountain State Art and Craft Fair features Appalachian art and music, particularly of West Virginia. Nearly 200 craftspeople exhibit and sell their handiwork, including chairs, quilts, weavings, paintings, photographs, leatherwork, and toys. Each day artists demonstrate weaving, lace making, silhouette art, antique printing, and shingle splitting. Folk musicians play Appalachian tunes on dulcimers, banjos, and fiddles; dancers clog and square dance; and storytellers spin Appalachian tales. Among the mountain foods served are barbecued chicken, corn bread and beans, roasted corn, and homemade ice cream.

Admission: adults, $4; children ages 6–12, $1; senior citizens, $3; members of tour groups, $3.
Location: Cedar Lakes Conference Center.
Directions: take I-77 Exit 132, and follow signs.
Information: Mountain State Art and Craft Fair, (304) 372-7000.
Tourist Information: Parkersburg-Wood County Convention and Visitors Bureau, (800) 752-4982 or (304) 428-1130.

Pocahontas County Pioneer Days
Marlinton, W.Va., Independence Day week.

One of the contests at Pocahontas County Pioneer Days tests men's skill at knife and tomahawk throwing; another finds the draft horse team that can pull the most weight. The Liar's Contest challenges contestants to tell the tallest tale. Children can enter contests to see how well they can eat crackers and then whistle, dress up as a hobo or clown, or prod their frog to jump the farthest. Parents can race their baby in the Diaper Derby or use their imagination to create the most unusual diaper. Homemakers can enter their best sewing project, most beautiful flower arrangement, or favorite bread, cake, jam, home-cured ham, or other dish in competition. Drivers can crash their cars in the Demolition Derby or try to maneuver the Mud Bog in their monster trucks. There's a contest for everyone.

The Pocahontas County Pioneer Days runs through Fourth of July week. Churches and social clubs put on ham and biscuit dinners or sell corn dogs, chili, and baked goods. The porch of the First National Bank is the stage for gospel, bluegrass, square dancing, and other performances, and there are hymn sings at the churches. Past festivals have had pig racing on Third Avenue several times during the week. There is also a flea market, an arts and crafts show, parades, a queen pageant, and an antique car show.

Admission: $2 for badge.

Location: downtown.

Information: Pioneer Days Association, (304) 799-4315.

Tourist Information: Pocahontas County Tourism Commission, (800) 336-7009 or (304) 799-4636.

Summerfest

Huntington, W. Va., last full week of July.

Summerfest is part of the Tri-State Fair and Regatta, a series of summer events in West Virginia, Ohio, and Kentucky. Held at Harris Riverfront Park on the Ohio River, Summerfest features evening concerts by well-known groups from the 1960s and 1970s. Past performers have included SteppenWolf, Gary Puckett and the Union Gap, Cornelius Brothers and Sister Rose, Sha-Na-Na, Bachman Turner Overdrive, and Blood, Sweat and Tears. The other festival highlight is the regatta, with races on the Ohio. Past Summerfests have hosted the Budweiser World Point Jet-Ski Race and the Miller Genuine Draft Classic Marathon National

Championship, with 150 powerboats racing in various classes. The week also offers remote-control car races, a bicycle tour, an antique car show, the Tri-State 10-kilometer race, carnival rides, hot-air balloons, and arts and crafts. About 400,000 people attend Summerfest, which runs for 10 days from Friday through the next Sunday, the last full week in July. Hours generally are evenings during the week and all day on the weekends.

Admission: free.
Location: Harris Riverfront Park.
Information: Tri-State Fair and Regatta, (304) 525-8141.
Tourist Information: Cabell-Huntington Convention and Visitors Bureau, (800) 635-6329 or (304) 525-7333.

Upper Ohio Valley Italian Festival
Wheeling, W. Va., fourth full weekend in July.

The Upper Ohio Valley Italian Festival celebrates the Italian heritage of the West Virginia panhandle and is one of the biggest festivals in the area. Spread along six blocks of Market Street in downtown Wheeling, the three-day event offers continuous entertainment on three stages, over 100 food and wine booths, arts and crafts, kiddie rides, and boccie and morra competitions. The entertainment schedule includes two headline acts Friday and Saturday evening, ethnic dancers, and strolling musicians. Past headliners have included Damian and the duet Toscano and Steritti. The festival runs all day Friday and Saturday, and morning and afternoon on Sunday.

Admission: free.
Location: Market Street between 10th and 16th streets.
Information: McClure House Hotel, (304) 233-1090.
Tourist Information: Wheeling Convention and Visitors Bureau, (800) 828-3097 or (304) 233-7709.

August

Maryland

Rocky Gap Country Music Festival
Cumberland, Md., first weekend in August.

High in the mountains of western Maryland, Rocky Gap State Park is the site of this annual country music festival, which mixes clogging, bluegrass, country, gospel, and folk. About 50,000 people attend the weekend event to hear big names like Johnny Cash, Roy Clark, Ricky Van Shelton, and Loretta Lynn, plus many local performers. The festival runs Friday evening through Sunday evening and also offers participatory workshops, folk music history, sing-alongs, musical instruction, and an arts and crafts village. Swimming, boating, and picnicking are available in the 3,200-acre Rocky Gap State Park.

Admission: adults, $15 per day; children, $1 per day; early-bird and weekend tickets available.
Location: Rocky Gap State Park.
Information: McClarran & Williams, (301) 724-2511.
Tourist Information: Allegany County Tourism, (301) 777-5967.

Harford County Seafood Festival
Havre de Grace, Md., second weekend in August.

Havre de Grace sits where the Susquehanna River enters the Chesapeake Bay, and the Harford County Seafood Festival offers the local catch and other seafood. The à la carte menu includes steamed crabs and shrimp, crab cakes, crab soup, seafood kabobs, soft-shell crabs, blackened redfish, Cajun spiced shrimp, seafood gumbo, and lobster. The feast also includes corn on the cob, a variety of salads, barbecued chicken, sandwiches, beer, and soft drinks. The good food can be enjoyed with entertainment, which in the past has included the Sweet Adelines, the Silver Eagle Cloggers, and other local groups. The festival includes arts and crafts and children's activities. It runs through the afternoon and evening on Saturday and all afternoon on Sunday.

Admission: $3; children 12 and under, free with adult.
Location: Tydings Park.
Information: Harford County Education Association, (410) 272-8349.
Tourist Information: Harford County Tourism, (410) 879-2000 ext. 339 or (301) 838-6000 ext. 339.

Leitersburg Peach Festival

Leitersburg, Md., second weekend in August.

The village of Leitersburg is in peach country, and at the Peach Festival community groups serve homemade peach pie, locally made peach ice cream, peach cobbler, peach jelly, and raw peaches by the bushel. The fire company cooks open-pit beef, and the Ladies' Auxiliary makes country ham sandwiches. Each afternoon a bluegrass band plays on the park's stage. The festival also offers pony rides, Civil War reenactments, arts and crafts, and a quilt raffle. The Homemakers Club judges the pie-baking contest and auctions off the winning pie.

Admission: free.
Location: Leitersburg Ruritan Community Park.
Directions: from Hagerstown follow Route 60 north for six miles.
Information: Leitersburg Ruritan Club, (301) 797-6387.
Tourist Information: Washington County Convention and Visitors Bureau, (800) 228-7829 or (301) 791-3246.

Selling peaches at the Leitersburg Peach Festival.

German Festival
Baltimore, Md., weekend in the middle of August.

Baltimore's German community has celebrated its heritage for more than 90 years, making the German Festival Baltimore's oldest ethnic festival. Now one the city's Showcase of Nations events, the festival offers three days of German music, dancing, food, and crafts in Carroll Park. Continuous entertainment scheduled each afternoon and evening has included the Edelweiss German Band, Die Alte Kameraden Band, the Bavarian Ambassadors, and other oompah bands. Vendors sell German beer, bratwurst, knockwurst, sauerkraut, and German pastries. The festival also includes German and Austrian crafts, beer steins, and souvenirs. It is sponsored by the Deutschamerikanischer Buergereverein von Maryland.

Admission: $2; children under 12 with adult, free.
Location: Carroll Park, Washington Boulevard and Monroe Street.

Information: Baltimore Area Visitors Center, (410) 837-4636 or
(800) 282-6632.
Tourist Information: Baltimore Area Convention and Visitors
Association, (410) 659-7300.

Maryland State Chili Championship and Crafts Show

Cumberland, Md., third weekend in August.

Chili cooks from all over the East Coast attend the Maryland
State Chili Championship, a sanctioned event of the International Chili Society. According to official rules, cooks may use
meats, chili peppers, and spices, but no beans. The cooks set up
their own booths, some elaborately decorated, and make the chili
from scratch using their own stoves and utensils. Each must
make a minimum of one gallon of chili, half of which goes to the
judges. After the winner is chosen, the rest of the chili is available
to festivalgoers for tasting.

The Maryland State Chili Championship runs Friday evening,
all day Saturday, and Sunday afternoon. Most activities, including the chili championship, are on Saturday. The festival also
features the Miss Chili Pepper crowning, arts and crafts, a street-
rod show, and country-and-western performances. There are also
contests in hot chili pepper eating, yelling, and having the best
chili belly.

Admission: free.
Location: Allegany County Fairgrounds.
Information: Maryland State Chili Championship, (301) 722-
5970.
Tourist Information: Allegany County Economic Development,
(301) 777-5967.

Williamsport C&O Canal Days

Williamsport, Md., fourth full weekend in August.

Williamsport, Maryland, celebrates its key location on the old
Chesapeake and Ohio (C & O) Canal with a weekend festival in

late August. In the heyday of the canal, the town had a canal aqueduct, a canal basin, a lockhouse and lock, and a lift bridge for the Pennsylvania Railroad. The National Park Service is restoring the canal as a recreational and historic resource, and Williamsport, whose fortunes have fluctuated with that of the canal, is benefiting.

Williamsport C & O Canal Days runs from Friday evening through Sunday afternoon. An ox-roast dinner, with spit-roasted beef, local corn on the cob, and coleslaw, is served Friday evening, followed by a street dance with a local country-and-western band. Through the weekend, entertainment is scheduled at Byron Park, and at the canal the National Park Service sponsors a bluegrass band that plays old canal songs. The festival also includes museum tours, guided canal walks, the Goodloe Byron 10-kilometer run, and a parade.

Admission: free.
Location: Byron Memorial Park and along the canal.
Information: Williamsport Town Office, (301) 223-7711.
Tourist Information: Washington County Tourism, (800) 228-7829 or (301) 791-3246.

Maryland Renaissance Festival

Annapolis, Md., weekends from last weekend in August to second weekend in October.

Sword swallowers, knights jousting in full armor, a court dinner with Henry VIII, a human chess game, mud-beggars, and comely wenches are some of the fun of this recreated village fair of sixteenth-century Tudor England. The Maryland Renaissance Festival also offers pipe organ music, magic, take-offs on Shakespeare, minstrels, and other entertainment on six stages. Authentically costumed craftspeople display and sell stained glass, sculpture, leatherwork, and clothing in the village craft shops. Even the food is from the Middle Ages, with steak on a stake, huge turkey drumsticks, meat pies, knave sandwiches, and mead, ale, and wine. The festival runs through the weekend, from late morning until early evening.

Admission: adults, $9.95; senior citizens, $8; students, $8; children, $3.50.
Location: Renaissance Festival grounds on Crownsville Road.
Directions: take Exit 5 off I-97; at third light turn right onto Crownsville Road and follow for 1.5 miles.
Information: Maryland Renaissance Festival, (800) 243-7304.
Tourist Information: Annapolis and Anne Arundel County Tourism Office, (410) 280-0445.

New York

New York Renaissance Festival

Tuxedo Park, N.Y., weekends from last weekend in July to third weekend in September.

See July—New York.

National Polka Festival

Hunter, N.Y., first weekend in August.

For four days, polka bands play and couples dance under the big tent at Hunter Mountain. The Polka Festival features bands from all over the United States, Canada, and Europe, playing the polkas of America and Eastern Europe. Five-time Grammy winner Jimmy Sturr is one of the top-name polka entertainers who have appeared. Other popular acts include the Polka Family, Lenny Gomulka and Chicago Push, Happy Louie, and Joe Stanky and His Cadets. Free polka lessons are offered each day, and talented couples can enter the National Polka Festival Dance Contest. The festival includes crowning of the Polka Queen, crafts, puppet shows, and Polish foods and beer. The festival runs afternoons and evenings Thursday through Sunday.

Admission: adults, $9; children 12 and under, $2.
Location: Hunter Mountain.

Directions: from Catskill, New York, follow Route 23A west for
    21 miles.
Information: Hunter Mountain Festivals, Ltd., (518) 263-3800.
Tourist Information: Greene County Promotion Department,
    (800) 542-2414 or (518) 943-3223.

Phelps Sauerkraut Festival

Phelps, N.Y., first weekend in August.

After his doctors advised him that seminary life would be too
rigorous for his frail health, Birton E. Babcock gave up hopes of
being a Presbyterian minister and in 1901 founded a sauerkraut
empire at Phelps, New York. Since then the town has become
known as the sauerkraut capital of the world, and as they say in
Phelps, sauerkraut is king. Since 1966 the town has celebrated
the pungent dish with midway rides, country music concerts, a
Saturday afternoon parade, a car show, a 20-kilometer road race,
chicken barbecues, and, of course, plenty of sauerkraut. A yearly
tradition is the ceremonial cutting of the chocolate sauerkraut
cake on Saturday evening, with the festival queen and other
dignitaries in attendance.

Admission: free.
Location: Phelps Firemen's Field, Ontario Street.
Information: Phelps Chamber of Commerce, (315) 548-5481.
Tourist Information: Ontario County Four Seasons, (800) 654-
    9798 (in N.Y.) or (716) 394-3915.

Spiedie Fest and Balloon Rally

Binghamton, N.Y., first weekend in August.

The Spiedie Fest and Balloon Rally celebrates spiedies, a local
delicacy of marinated meat or poultry barbecued on a skewer and
served on an Italian roll. Vendors sell spiedies through the weekend, and on Sunday spiedie cooks, each with his or her own
special recipe, participate in the Spiedie Cooking Contest. The

balloon rally draws some 40 balloon teams to Otsiningo Park for morning and evening launches, weather permitting. The festival also offers a volleyball tournament, a crafts fair, an antique car show, a petting zoo, and musical entertainment through the weekend, including rock bands, blues singers, jazz groups, and bluegrass bands. The festival runs from Friday evening through Sunday evening.

Admission: free.
Location: Otsiningo Park.
Information: American Cancer Society, (607) 722-6471.
Tourist Information: Broome County Convention and Visitors Bureau, (800) 836-6740 or (607) 772-8860.

Harlem Week

New York, N.Y., first Monday through the third Sunday in August.

Harlem is one of New York's oldest neighborhoods, settled in 1658 as the village of Nieuw Haarlem by the Dutch, and the first Afro-American families moved there in 1672. The neighborhood's interesting history and strong community spirit is celebrated in August with a two-week festival. Although the schedule of events changes from year to year, Harlem Week usually includes a jazz festival, with outdoor and indoor performances featuring rhythm and blues, reggae, bebop, calypso, a cappella, Dixieland, and Latin jazz. There is also an Afro-American film festival, a tristate high school basketball tournament, and historic tours of the neighborhood. Past festivals have also included antique auto shows, educational conferences, gospel concerts, and fine arts exhibitions. Harlem Week concludes on Sunday with Harlem Day, marked by a street festival in the heart of Harlem with four stages of entertainment, fashion shows, arts and crafts, and food.

Admission: free, charges for some events.
Location: various locations in Harlem and New York City.
Information: Harlem Visitors and Convention Association, (212) 427-3317.

Tourist Information: New York Convention and Visitors Bureau, (212) 397-8222.

Festival of North Country Folklife

Massena, N.Y., second Saturday in August.

Celebrating the folk culture of the St. Lawrence Valley and the Adirondacks, the Festival of North Country Folklife brings together musicians, storytellers, and craftspeople of the region. Musical performances demonstrate the traditions of French Canada, northern New York, and New England, with fiddlers, banjo pickers, and dulcimer players often performing songs originating in logging camps, country kitchens, and small-town dance halls. At the Talkers' Tent, local old-timers recount area history, tell tall tales of the Adirondacks, or demonstrate animal calls. North Country craftspeople demonstrate such things as Mohawk cornhusk work, rug weaving, fungus decorating, decoy carving, and Adirondack rustic furnituremaking. Food served includes some regional dishes like French-Canadian *tourtieres* (meat pies), pea soup, and traditional North Country chicken barbecue dinners. The festival runs all day Saturday.

Admission: adults, $1; senior citizens and students, $.50.
Information: Massena Chamber of Commerce, (315) 769-3525.
Tourist Information: 1000 Islands International Council, (800) 847-5263 or (315) 482-2520.

International Celtic Festival

Hunter, N.Y., weekend in the middle of August.

With Hunter Mountain rising above them, 400 bagpipers and drummers march en masse, playing an inspiring rendition of "Scotland the Brave." The International Celtic Festival celebrates the native music and dance of Ireland, Scotland, Wales, and Brittany, featuring performers from the United States and abroad. One popular returning group is Boru, direct from Dublin, playing

Irish folk songs and ballads. Other popular performers are Dermot Henry, an Irish master of blarney, and Pat Roper of Glasgow, Scotland. There are also Irish singers, Celtic bands, storytellers, sea-chantey singers, and Highland dancers. The festival includes pipe band competitions, folk dance competitions, sheep herding demonstrations, and food of the British Isles.

Admission: adults, $9; children 12 and under, $2.
Location: Hunter Mountain.
Directions: from Catskill, New York, follow Route 23A west for 21 miles.
Information: Hunter Mountain Festivals, Ltd., (518) 263-3800.
Tourist Information: Greene County Promotion Department, (800) 542-2414 or (518) 943-3223.

New York State Woodsmen's Field Days

Boonville, N.Y., third weekend in August.

Located on the edge of the Adirondacks, Boonville has long been a lumber town. At the New York State Woodsmen's Field Days, lumberjacks and lumberjills from across the state and throughout the Northeast test their modern and old-time lumberjack skills. There are contests in two-man crosscut sawing, one-man crosscut sawing, bow sawing, log rolling, tree felling, axe throwing, horizontal chopping, standing-block chopping, chainsawing, hydraulic loader skills, and skidding. During the three-day event, churches and clubs in Boonville cook steak-and-egg breakfasts, lasagna dinners, roast beef dinners, and chicken barbecues. The festival also includes an arts and crafts show, dancing at the VFW Hall, a best beards contest, and a noontime parade on Saturday that is followed by the coronation of the Miss Forest Queen.

Admission: adults, $4.50; children 12 and under, $3.
Location: Boonville-Oneida County Fairgrounds, Route 294, and other locations in Boonville.
Information: New York State Woodsmen's Field Days, Inc., (315) 942-4593.
Tourist Information: Oneida County Tourism, (800) 237-0100 (in N.Y.) or (800) 426-3132.

Polish Town U.S.A. Street Fair and Polka Festival

Riverhead, N.Y., third weekend in August.

Riverhead, "Polish Town U.S.A," celebrates its ethnic heritage with one of the biggest festivals on Long Island. The festival begins on Saturday morning with a traditional Polish Mass at St. Isidore's Roman Catholic Church. Past festivals have featured a reenactment of the Polish legend of the Trumpeteer of Krakow and a portrayal of an old-fashioned Polish wedding and wedding party customs. At the street festival, almost 200 booths, colorfully decorated in Polish style, offer Polish imports, crafts, and Polish food. Past entertainment has included the St. Maximilian Kolbe Polish Dance Group and polka music by the Rich Rudolph Orchestra. Held in the evening, the Polka Festival features Polish orchestras and polka dancing.

Admission: Street Fair, free; Polka Festival, adults, $10; children under 12, $5.

Information: Polish Town Civic Association, (516) 369-1616.

Tourist Information: Long Island Convention and Visitors Bureau, (800) 441-4601 or (516) 794-4222.

Pennsylvania

Pennsylvania Renaissance Faire

Manheim, Pa., last weekend in June through second weekend in October.

See June—Pennsylvania.

Bavarian Fun Fest

Sharon, Pa., last weekend in July, first weekend in August.

See July—Pennsylvania.

Fort Armstrong Folk Festival

Kittanning, Pa., first weekend in August.

Kittanning is the oldest town in western Pennsylvania, the site of Fort Armstrong during the French and Indian War. The community celebrates that heritage on the first weekend in August. A hundred craftspeople in period clothes demonstrate weaving, wool spinning, broom making, leather tooling, glassblowing, and other colonial skills. Entertainment is provided on two stages and includes folk music and dancing, as well as more modern pop, rock, and big-band sounds. The festival also offers a 10-kilometer run, a fine arts exhibit, and a variety of food. It runs evenings Wednesday through Friday and afternoons and evenings Saturday and Sunday.

Admission: free.
Location: Riverfront Park.
Information: Armstrong County YMCA, (412) 543-6363.
Tourist Information: Armstrong County Tourist Bureau, (412) 548-3226.

Pittsburgh Three Rivers Regatta

Pittsburgh, Pa., first weekend in August.

Pittsburgh's landmark Point Park, where the Allegheny and Monongahela rivers become the Ohio, is the location for one of the country's biggest river regattas. The International Outboard Grand Prix is the highlight of the weekend, with some of the most talented powerboat drivers of the world competing for $25,000 in prize money. Other water events include exhibition water skiing, an Anything That Floats Race, and a Night Lighted Boat Parade.

The Regatta generally runs from Thursday through Sunday, with most activities on the weekend. Each evening, nationally acclaimed entertainers perform at the festival's main stage. Other activities include a parade, an air show, and a hare-and-hounds balloon race. Some 600,000 people attend the Three Rivers Regatta.

Admission: free.
Location: Point Park.
Information: The Carson Group, (412) 471-1900.
Tourist Information: Pittsburgh Convention and Visitors Bureau, (800) 366-0093 or (412) 281-7711.

Chester County Old Fiddlers' Picnic

Coatesville, Pa., second Saturday in August.

At the Old Fiddlers' Picnic, bluegrass, country-and-western, and "old-timey music" players take their turn at the open stage. From about 10 a.m. until 8 p.m., solo acts (taking not more than 10 minutes) and groups (taking not more than 20 minutes) play fiddle, banjo, guitar, dulcimer, and unusual instruments like wheel fiddle, record, and washtub bass. Often, while waiting to go on stage, musicians gather beneath the park's trees to jam; sometimes an impromptu band forms and an audience gathers to listen.

The Chester County Old Fiddlers' Picnic has been held since 1923. It runs on a Saturday from midmorning until night and also offers two square dances during the day, hayrides, homemade crafts, and festival foods. Visitors are invited to bring their instruments and join the fun.

Admission: $4 per vehicle.
Location: Hibernia County Park.
Directions: from Coatesville follow Pa. Route 82 north 2 miles; turn left on and follow Cedar Knoll Road for 1.25 miles to Hibernia Park.
Information: Chester County Parks and Recreation Department, (215) 344-6415.
Tourist Information: Chester County Tourist Bureau, (800) 228-9933 or (215) 344-6365.

Lebanon Bologna Fest

Lebanon, Pa., second full weekend in August.

In the early 1800s German settlers in the Lebanon Valley first made the now-famous Lebanon bologna, a sausagelike bologna made of meats and herbs. Today a three-day festival celebrates the local luncheon meat. Lebanon, sweet, and ring bologna—plus a variety of dishes using them—are served. Community groups also serve local Pennsylvania Dutch dishes. There is continuous entertainment on three stages in the afternoon and evening Friday, Saturday, and Sunday. Much of the music is folk or country, and popular bands like the Charley Daniels Band or Lee Greenwood are usually scheduled. Other activities include the crowning of the Bologna Fest Queen, hot-air balloon launches, local crafts, and an antique car show.

Admission: ages 11 and over, $3; ages 3–10, $2.
Location: Lebanon Area Fairgrounds.
Information: Lebanon Valley Tourist and Visitors Bureau, (717) 272-8555.

Shadyside Summer Arts Festival

Pittsburgh, Pa., second weekend in August.

The Shadyside Arts Festival is geared to serious art and music lovers. More than 200 artists and designers of American collectibles exhibit their work in the juried show. The festival includes conventional two- and three-dimensional artwork as well as novelties such as neon art. A highlight of the event is Art in Process, where artists demonstrate and explain their techniques. The art show runs through the afternoon and evening Friday, Saturday, and Sunday. The audio portion of the festival consists of nightly jazz performances on two stages. Out-of-town musicians have included Red Rodney, Jay McShain, Ben Sidrin, and Bob Mintzer.

Admission: free.
Location: Walnut Street business district.
Information: Shadyside Summer Arts Festival, (412) 681-2809.
Tourist Information: Pittsburgh Convention and Visitors Bureau, (800) 366-0093 or (412) 281-7711.

Goschenhoppen Folk Festival

East Greenville, Pa., second Friday and Saturday in August.

The Goschenhoppen Folk Festival is an authentic demonstration of eighteenth- and nineteenth-century Pennsylvania Dutch life, particularly in the Goschenhoppen region of southeastern Pennsylvania. The Goschenhoppen Historians, who put on the event, are so strict that the festival's craftspeople, musicians, and lecturers wear authentic period clothing and vendors sell only Pennsylvania German foods—no pizza, hamburgers, or Cokes. The group carefully researches all aspects of the festival and is determined to prevent any inaccuracy: if a man cannot be found to demonstrate weaving, that skill is eliminated because only men were weavers in the Goschenhoppen region.

The festival is held in a 10-acre, tree-shaded picnic grove and runs Friday afternoon and evening and Saturday all day. More than 500 skilled and apprentice craftspeople use authentic tools to demonstrate more than 150 crafts, including horseshoeing, blacksmithing, butchering, fraktur (German calligraphic script),

Artisan at the Goschenhoppen Folk Festival.

wheelwrighting, and hatmaking. Beggars, peddlars, and other itinerants in appropriate costumes roam the grounds, asking for food or offering cure-all liniments. Visitors can taste old-fashioned foods like lima bean pie, fresh buttermilk, corn pie, pickled red-beet eggs, peppermint water, and a ham-and-bean dinner.

Admission: adults, $5; children under 12, free.
Location: New Goschenhoppen Park on Third Street.
Information: Goschenhoppen Historians, Inc., (215) 234-8953.
Tourist Information: Valley Forge Convention and Visitors Bureau, (800) 441-3549 or (215) 278-3558.

We Love Erie Days

Erie, Pa., weekend in the middle of August.

Erie is home port for the brig US *Niagara*, the flagship of Commodore Oliver Hazard Perry in his victory over the British in the Battle of Lake Erie during the War of 1812. The *Niagara* and modern navy and coast guard ships are docked at Erie's waterfront and are open for public tours during We Love Erie Days. The festival celebrates Erie's Great Lakes heritage and includes sailboat racing, a tugboat parade, and cruises on Lake Erie and Presque Isle Bay. A variety of entertainment is scheduled during the four-day event, including evening headliner performances, sky-diving demonstrations, and a Sunday-night fireworks show. Past festivals have offered a 10-kilometer race, a video game tournament, and a bus "roadeo."

Admission: free.
Location: downtown and at the waterfront.
Information: Erie Area Chamber of Commerce, (814) 454-7191.

San Rocco Festa

Aliquippa, Pa., weekend closest to August 16.

After Mass at St. Titus Roman Catholic Church on Sunday morning, a one-mile-long procession passes through neighboring streets in Aliquippa. Thirty men dressed in white robes carry the church's statue of San Rocco in a wooden cupola dressed with chiambelli, a symbolic Italian sweetbread. Men, women, and children follow the statue singing religious and Italian songs. Along the way people hug each other and say "Viva San Rocco!"

San Rocco, who died 600 years ago, is venerated in the Roman Catholic Church as protector against the plague and all contagious diseases. The San Rocco Festa began centuries ago in Patrica, Italy, where San Rocco cured the sick with his prayers. Emigrants from Patrica who began new lives in Aliquippa continued the San Rocco tradition and have held the festival every year since 1925.

This Italian festival begins Friday evening and continues through Saturday and Sunday, with Italian entertainment and food all weekend. There are contests for the best homemade wine and homemade spaghetti sauce, and competitions in boccie (Italian bowling), morra (an Italian counting game), dancing the tarantella, and spaghetti eating. On Saturday morning a priest performs the blessing of the dogs.

Admission: free.

Location: Grand Avenue and Sheffield Terrace.

Information: Beaver County Tourist Promotion Agency, (412) 728-0212.

Unity Weekend

Philadelphia, Pa., third weekend in August.

Celebrating family unity and Afro-American culture, Unity Weekend attracts more than half a million people for three days of events. Most of the action is on Sunday, Unity Day, when crowds fill the Benjamin Franklin Parkway in downtown Philadelphia. Continuous entertainment is scheduled on six stages, including a jazz and reggae stage, a kids' stage, a gospel stage, and a fitness stage. Performers are both local and nationally known. The soul, African, and Caribbean food served includes such things as barbecued ribs, Jamaican curried goat, and bean pie. Several pavilions offer art shows, environmental education, and African heritage exhibits. One purpose of the festival is to make the public aware of community resources, so more than 200 organizations set up information booths on the parkway. The weekend also includes a celebrity softball game, a chess tournament, a 10-kilometer run, neighborhood cleanups, and special concerts.

Admission: free.

Location: Benjamin Franklin Parkway and other locations in Philadelphia.

Information: Minority Media, WDAS, (215) 581-2100.

Tourist Information: Philadelphia Convention and Visitors Bureau, (800) 321-9563 or (215) 636-1666.

Musikfest

Bethlehem, Pa., begins third Saturday in August and continues for nine days.

With over 600 performances by over 230 individuals and musical groups, Musikfest is one of the largest performing arts events in the country. Held in Bethlehem, a German Moravian settlement with a 250-year history of fine music, the festival offers a wide selection, including jazz, polka, classical, bluegrass, folk, chamber, big-band, rock, and choral music.

During the nine days, the festival is centered downtown in a historic district with the largest collection of German colonial architecture in the United States. Eight plazas, or Plätze, offer food, music, and activities reflecting a theme. For instance, Americaplatz features performances of bluegrass, jazz, and big-band music and such foods as Chesapeake Bay crab cakes, barbecued ribs, and other American specialties. Festplatz, with a German theme, offers visitors a chance to listen to German oompah bands, participate in the Chicken Dance, and enjoy a bratwurst platter. Familienplatz and Kinderplatz offer special activities for families and children, including crafts, puppet shows, and storytelling. The festival also has several concert series featuring performances of classical, jazz, chamber, and sacred music.

The variety and quality of the performances is outstanding. Past Musikfests have included the Daisy Jug Band; the Woody Herman Orchestra; the Reading Community Gospel Choir; the town band of Perg, Austria; the Bruce Daigrepont Cajun Band from Louisiana; the Moravian Trombone Choir; and German classical pianist Konrad Elser. Kunstplatz, the main stage of the festival, features star performers, who in the past have included Marie Osmond, Livingston Taylor, and the Sammy Kaye Orchestra.

Admission: free, except for some indoor events.
Location: downtown historic area.
Information: Bethlehem Musikfest Association, (215) 861-0678.
Tourist Information: Lehigh Valley Convention and Visitors Bureau, (800) 747-0561 or (215) 266-0560.

Philadelphia Folk Festival

Schwenksville, Pa., weekend prior to Labor Day weekend.

The Philadelphia Folk Festival is the oldest continuously running eclectic folk festival in the United States. Begun in 1962, it has featured virtually all American folk musicians of note. Performers have included Arlo Guthrie, David Bromberg, Judy Collins, Joan Baez, John Denver, Pete Seeger, Ritchie Havens, Merle Travis, the Texas Cowboys, Tom Paxton, John Hartford, Steve Goodman, and John Pryne. There are evening concerts Friday through Sunday and afternoon concerts Saturday and Sunday. A showcase of new talent is featured Friday afternoon, and workshops are offered on three stages Saturday and Sunday. The festival also includes craftspeople demonstrating their work and community groups selling food. Camping is available at the festival site, and after the evening concerts there are campfire sings in the campground.

Admission: various price, starting with advance one-day adult ticket at $13.
Location: Old Poole Farm, Upper Salford.
Directions: from Schwenksville follow festival signs.
Information: Philadelphia Folk Festival, (800) 556-3655 or (215) 242-0150.
Tourist Information: Valley Forge Convention and Visitors Bureau, (800) 441-3549 or (215) 278-3558.

German dancers at Bethlehem's Musikfest.

Corn Festival

Shippensburg, Pa., last Saturday in August.

Shippensburg sits in the middle of corn country, and corn is served all ways at the Corn Festival: corn on the cob, corn dogs, hush puppies, corn fritters, chicken corn soup, popcorn, and corn muffins. Celebrating the summer harvest, the festival features local entertainers, performing on stage and strolling through the crowd, and a crafts show with more than 250 exhibitors, some demonstrating their work. The day's activities also include a 6 a.m. breakfast, a biathlon, a classic car show, and children's entertainment. Shippensburg is considered the second oldest town west of the Susquehanna River, and the festival benefits historic preservation projects.

Admission: free.
Location: downtown streets.
Information: Corn Festival Organization, (717) 530-1390.

Tourist Information: Cumberland Valley Visitors' Council, (717) 261-1200.

Virginia

Festival of Nations

Norfolk, Va., weekend in July or August.

See July—Virginia.

Virginia Highlands Festival

Abingdon, Va., last weekend of July and first two weeks in August.

See July—Virginia.

Elkton Field Day

Elkton, Va., first week in August.

Since 1908, Elkton's homecoming has been Elkton Field Day—which now runs a whole week. Originally a day of jousting, baseball games, greased pig chases, sack races, and other rural athletic events, the festival now features carnival rides, beauty pageants, a giant parade, and even some of the old-time events like hog calling, husband calling, and awards for the longest married couple, the largest family present, and the person who came the longest distance. Entertainment includes country, bluegrass, gospel, and clog dancing groups from all over Virginia. Among the regional foods served are southern deep-fried chicken and Virginia-cured ham sandwiches. The festival runs through the evening Tuesday through Friday and all day Saturday.

Admission: free.
Location: Blue Ridge Park.

Information: Junior Order of United American Mechanics, (703) 298-2225.

Tourist Information: Shenandoah Valley Travel Association, (703) 740-3132.

Old Fiddlers' Convention

Galax, Va., second weekend in August.

For more than 50 years, the Moose Lodge in Galax, Virginia, has put on a bluegrass and old-time music festival. When it was first held in 1935, the Old Fiddlers' Convention drew some 1,300 people, many arriving in Galax on foot or in horse-drawn wagons. Now more than 30,000 people attend, and the more than 1,500 contestants come from 31 states and half a dozen foreign countries, including Japan, Australia, and England. In fact, a Japanese performer won the mandolin competition one year.

Minstrel singer at Leesburg, Virginia's August Court Days.

Despite the changes, the Old Fiddlers' Convention is still an authentic small-town bluegrass festival. The only electronics allowed are the on-stage sound system, and only music in the public domain, such as "Turkey in the Straw," can be performed. The Moose Club donates $10,000 in prize money for the following categories: guitar, bluegrass fiddle, bluegrass banjo, mandolin, dulcimer, auto harp, dobro, old-time band, and clog and flat-foot dancing. Although the festival is scheduled for evenings Wednesday through Friday and the afternoon and evening on Saturday, much of the action takes place after hours and off stage in informal jam sessions held amid the campers and pickup trucks in the parking area. Often the playing continues until dawn.

Admission: $6.
Location: Felts Park.
Information: Galax-Carroll-Grayson Chamber of Commerce, (703) 236-2184.

Natural Chimneys Jousting Tournament
Mt. Solon, Va., third Saturday in August.

America's oldest continuously held sporting event is not the Kentucky Derby, but the Natural Chimneys Jousting Tournament at Mt. Solon, Virginia. The contest has been held each year since 1821, when two men jousted to settle who would have a local woman as his bride. Today's participants don't race toward each other, attempting to injure or knock the other from his horse. Riders now individually race down a 90-yard course, aiming their lance toward three steel rings suspended from crossbars. The old event is made more colorful by the 120-foot limestone "chimneys" towering above the open greensward. Regional foods are served, and bluegrass music is performed in the evening.

Admission: $3.
Location: Natural Chimneys Regional Park, Virginia Route 731.
Information: Natural Chimneys Regional Park, (703) 350-2510.
Tourist Information: Shenandoah Valley Travel Association, (703) 740-3132.

Town Point Jazz Festival
Norfolk, Va., usually third weekend in August.

At the Town Point Jazz Festival, crowds sit on the grass at Norfolk's waterfront, watching passing boats in the harbor and enjoying the sounds of local and nationally known jazz artists. Past festivals have featured Dizzy Gillespie, Doc Severinsen, Spyro Gyra, Stanley Jorden, Roy Ayers, and Ramsey Lewis. The festival kicks off with a local group and a national group Friday evening. Saturday afternoon and evening features three or four groups. The festival ends on Sunday afternoon with two or three more performances. Food and drink are available.

Admission: free.
Location: Town Point Park.
Information: Festevents, Ltd., (804) 627-7809.
Tourist Information: Norfolk Convention and Visitors Bureau, (804) 441-5266.

August Court Days
Leesburg, Va., third weekend in August.

In the mid-1700s the Loudoun County judicial court held session every three months. The mid-August session, scheduled during the local farmers' break between planting and harvest, was celebrated with a street fair, entertainment, and much merrymaking. Today, Leesburg citizens relive the excitement of court day when the streets of the historic district are blocked to traffic and filled with crafts booths, roving entertainers, and local civic organizations offering a wide selection of foods. A stage, set up in front of the courthouse, has featured such groups as Professor Tuckahoe's Minstrels, the Ebenezer String Band, and Fearless Airborne Conjury.

The festival begins each morning when the town crier walks through Leesburg announcing the day's events and declaring "Hear ye, hear ye! August Court Days begins!" Each day, local actors reenact a court drama of 200 years ago, the town gossip is

Wine tasting at the Virginia Festival.

dunked on the courthouse green, and jugglers entertain on the streets. One hundred artisans show such things as jewelry, quilts, pottery, stenciling, and period reproduction furniture; they are also expected to spend 50 percent of their time demonstrating their craft. August Court Days runs Saturday and Sunday morning and afternoon.

Admission: $4; children under 12, free.

Location: King and Market streets.

Information: Loudoun County Tourist Information Center, (800) 752-6118 or (703) 777-0519.

Virginia Wine Festival
Middleburg, Va., weekend of last Saturday in August.

Thomas Jefferson, well-versed in European wines, saw the potential for wine growing in his home state. Today his dream is a reality, with some 45 wineries prospering in the northern and central parts of Virginia. More than 25 of those establishments set up booths at the Virginia Wine Festival, one of the longest-running wine festivals on the East Coast. The $12 admission fee to the event provides a commemorative wineglass for tasting each winery's selection. Bottles and cases of wines are for sale.

The two-day event is held at Great Meadow, a 400-acre tract of fields and woodlands, the site of the Virginia and the International Gold Cup Steeplechase races. Vendors sell a variety of ethnic and American foods, which can be enjoyed while listening to a Dixieland band or sitting beside Great Meadow's lake. The festival also includes cork-throwing contests, waiters' races, grape stomping, and seminars on wine tasting, matching wine and food, and wine growing. It runs from late morning through the afternoon both Saturday and Sunday.

Admission: $12; children under 16, free.
Location: Great Meadow Park.
Directions: from The Plains exit of I-66 (Exit 8), follow Route 245 south for 1 mile.
Information: Vinifera Wine Growers Association, (703) 754-8564.
Tourist Information: Loudoun County Tourist Information Center, (703) 777-0519.

West Virginia

Augusta Festival
Elkins, W.Va., second weekend in August.

The Augusta Festival, which follows the summer Augusta Heritage Arts Workshops at Davis and Elkins College, offers performances by many of the nationally known folk artists who teach

Jam session at the Augusta Festival's Pickin' Tent.

the workshops. Much of the program features Appalachian folk art, with storytelling, clogging, dulcimer playing, and fiddling, but other cultures are often represented. Concerts and square dances are scheduled Friday and Saturday evening, and a day of activities is held on Saturday under the century-old oak trees in the Elkins City Park. Artists perform through the morning and afternoon at five locations, including a storytelling tent, a kids' tent, and a pickin' tent, where everyone is invited to join an all-day jam session. There are also workshops, a juried craft show, exhibits, and food.

Admission: evening concerts, $10; weekend, $17; seniors and children 12 and under, half price; children 5 and under, free.

Location: Davis and Elkins College and Elkins City Park.

Information: Augusta Heritage Center, (304) 636-1903.

Tourist Information: Randolph County Convention and Visitors Bureau, (800) 422-3304 or (304) 636-2717.

Charleston Sternwheel Regatta

Charleston, W.Va., nine days preceding Labor Day.

Grand sternwheel paddleboats, some three stories tall and more than 100 feet long, race to the finish line on the Kanawha River at Charleston. The boats come from the Kanawha, the Ohio, and the Mississippi, and many have been restored to riverboat style. Another highlight of the festival adds to the Mississippi riverboat atmosphere: a Dixieland jazz band leads a New Orleans funeral parade of costumed "mourners" singing and dancing through the streets of Charleston.

The Charleston Sternwheel Regatta runs for 10 days from Saturday to Labor Day and is considered the largest river festival east of the Mississippi. Other activities include athletic tournaments, the West Virginia Clogging and Hoedown Championship, a Grand Feature Parade, river cruises, the Kanawha River Powerboat Race, a hot-air balloon race, a restaurant festival, skydiving exhibitions, and a towboat "pushers and shovers" contest. Free evening performances, held on the levee, have featured Michael McDonald, the Georgia Satellites, and Billy Preston. The Sternwheel Regatta Races are held the last Sunday of the festival.

Admission: free.

Location: downtown at City Levee.

Information: Charleston Festival Commission, (304) 348-6419.

Tourist Information: Charleston Convention and Visitors Bureau, (800) 733-5469 or (304) 344-5075.

September

Delaware

Nanticoke Indian Powwow
Millsboro, Del., weekend after Labor Day.

The Nanticoke tribe first encountered Europeans in 1608, when Captain John Smith explored the Chesapeake Bay. The English began settling the Delmarva Peninsula after 1624, when Charles I claimed the land for the crown. For a while the Nanticoke coexisted with the new settlers, but eventually conflicts developed. In 1642, Maryland governor Cecil Calvert declared war on the Nanticoke, beginning 26 years of official harassment of the tribe. In 1668, the Nanticoke succumbed, and Chief Unnacokasimmon signed a peace treaty that took away all of their rights. Many of the Nanticoke left to join other tribes farther west, and some moved north to present-day Delaware, where they settled on the Indian River.

Each September, the Nanticoke now living in southern Delaware host a powwow for mostly East Coast tribes, including Lenape, Cherokee, and Seminole. Ceremonial and intertribal dancing in full regalia is scheduled each afternoon; native American craftspeople demonstrate silverwork, beadwork, and leatherwork; and a chief's son tells stories. The Nanticoke and other groups serve foods like fried bread, corn and beans, and Indian tacos, and native American traders from across the country sell crafts and artwork. The festival is held at the Nanticoke Indian Museum, established in 1980 in an old Nanticoke Indian school.

Admission: parking, $5.

Location: Nanticoke Indian Museum, Route 24.
Information: Nanticoke Indian Museum, (302) 945-7022 or (302) 945-3400.
Tourist Information: Millsboro Chamber of Commerce, (302) 934-8171.

Oktoberfest

Newark, Del., third weekend in September.

The Delaware Saengerbund, the state's oldest German-American club, recreates on its grounds the famous autumn festival that has been held in Bavaria since 1810. Under a big circus tent, the festival offers authentic German sausages, sauerkraut, potato salad, and beer. From its opening Friday evening until it closes on Sunday evening, the festival features continuous German bands for dancing plus performances by Bavarian dance groups. Jacob Titz and his Alpine Band are a regular on Saturday night.

Admission: persons 21 and older, $5; under 21, $3.
Location: Delaware Saengerbund grounds, 49 Salem Church Road.
Directions: located near intersection of routes 4 and 273.
Information: Delaware Saengerbund, (302) 366-8868.
Tourist Information: Greater Wilmington Convention and Visitors Bureau, (800) 422-1181 or (302) 654-4088.

Maryland and the District of Columbia

Maryland Renaissance Festival

Annapolis, Md., weekends from last weekend in August to second weekend in October.

See August—Maryland.

National Hard Crab Derby and Fair

Crisfield, Md., Labor Day Weekend.

The National Hard Crab Derby got its start in 1947 when crab packers in Crisfield dumped a basket of blue crabs on Main Street and awarded a prize to the owner of the crab that climbed out of the pile first. Today, over 300 crabs compete, and a Governor's Cup Race features crabs representing many of the 50 states. For both the Derby and the Governor's Cup, crabs are placed in individual gates. When the gun is fired, the gates are tipped downward, sending the racers onto a sloped platform. The first to cross the bottom edge is the winner.

The crab races are held Saturday afternoon, but there are activities from Friday evening through Sunday. The Crab Picking Contest is usually held just before the Governor's Cup. The contestants, mostly professionals from the local processing plants, compete to pull the most meat out of a pile of crabs in 15 minutes. Other activities include a Miss Crustacean Beauty Contest, a crab-cooking contest, a boat-docking contest, a street parade, arts and crafts, and entertainment. There is plenty of fresh, local seafood, such as soft-shelled crab sandwiches, crab cakes, and spicy steamed crabs.

Admission: adults, $3.
Location: Somers Cove Marina.
Information: Derby and Fair Association, Inc., (410) 968-2682.
Tourist Information: Somerset County Tourism, (410) 651-2968.

Adams Morgan Day

Washington, D.C., usually Sunday of first full weekend in September.

Adams Morgan, Washington's most ethnic neighborhood and its busiest restaurant district, celebrates good eating and cultural diversity with this one-day street festival. More than a quarter-million people fill 18th Street, enjoying musical entertainment

African drummers perform at Adams Morgan Day.

and rows of food booths representing the neighborhood's cultural mix. The event is known as the biggest block party of the East Coast.

Adams Morgan Day runs Sunday afternoon and early evening. Nearly five blocks of booths sell arts, crafts, and foods of many cultures: Mexican, African, American, Australian, Italian, Hawaiian, Korean, Caribbean, Brazilian, Panamanian, Cajun, and Bolivian. Music abounds on five stages, offering rhythm and blues, zydeco, Latin, and rock. One of the stages is devoted to gospel music, another to dance.

Admission: free.

Location: 18th Street between Columbia Road and Florida Avenue in the Adams Morgan neighborhood.

Information: Adams Morgan Day, (202) 332-3292.

Tourist Information: Washington, D.C., Convention and Visitors Association, (202) 789-7000.

Labor Day Skipjack Races and Land Festival

Deal Island, Md., Sunday and Monday of Labor Day weekend.

For more than 30 years, America's last working sailboats, the skipjacks, have raced off Deal Island on Labor Day. Beginning at 9 a.m. the skipjacks and four classes of yachts head out on a 12-mile course, much of it within view of Deal Island Harbor. Another highlight of the day is the boat-docking competition of commercial motorboats. Teams and individuals compete to securely dock their boats in the least amount of time. The land festival that runs both days includes a parade on Sunday, canoe and swimming races, country-and-western music, arts and crafts, and Maryland seafood.

Admission: $2; children under 12, free.
Location: Deal Island Harbor.
Information: Deal Island-Chance Lions Club, (410) 784-2428.
Tourist Information: Somerset County Tourism, (410) 651-2968.

Sunfest

Ocean City, Md., Thursday through Sunday after Labor Day.

Ocean City's end-of-summer fling is its most popular festival, attracting as many as 200,000 people. The four-day event offers arts and crafts, a variety of entertainment, and food, including Eastern Shore specialties: crab cakes, soft crab sandwiches, clam fritters, smoked fish, Maryland cream of crab soup, and raw clams and oysters. Sunfest opens Thursday morning with a march of the Struttin' Mummers down the boardwalk.

From Thursday through Sunday, a wide range of music is performed under a big-top tent, including bluegrass, country, barbershop, organ music, and jazz. Performers have included the First U.S. Army Band, the Phillips Ragtime Band, Country Grass, and Dancing By Kids, Inc. One popular event is the Treasure

Hunt, where a local jeweler buries $7,500 of jewels in 75 pouches in the sand and contestants have a hour to dig them up. Other regular events include an old-fashioned bathing suit contest, a fishing tournament, and a kite festival.

Admission: free.
Location: Inlet Parking Lot and Beach.
Information: Ocean City Public Relations Office, (800) 626-2326.
Tourist Information: Worcester County Tourism, (410) 289-8181.

Maryland Seafood Festival

Annapolis, Md., second weekend in September.

First held in 1967, the Maryland Seafood Festival offers such goodies as steamed crabs, softshell crabs, seafood gumbo, crab fluff, steamed shrimp, soft clams, mussels in wine sauce, and crab cakes—much of it from the Chesapeake. The festival runs afternoons and evenings Friday, Saturday, and Sunday. Continuous entertainment on stage has included big bands, country-and-western groups, and classic rock performers. Children can enjoy treasure hunts, crab races, and sand sculpting on the beach. Clowns, mimes, and magicians wander through the crowd. Often there are special demonstrations by the Maryland National Guard and the police K-9 team.

Admission: adults, $5; children under 12, free with adult.
Location: Sandy Point State Park.
Information: Greater Annapolis Chamber of Commerce, (410) 268-7676.
Tourist Information: Annapolis and Anne Arundel County Tourism Office, (410) 280-0445.

Irish Festival

Baltimore, Md., weekend in the middle of September.

Baltimore's Irish Festival begins Friday evening with a concert by a top-name Irish musician; one year it was Tommy Makem, well known for his banjo renditions of popular Irish tunes. The festival offers continuous Irish music through the afternoon and evening Saturday and Sunday; past performers have included Billy McComiskey, the Rigadoo Irish Band, the Amhrani Na Gaelige Chorale, and the Rosin Dubh Dancers. There is also a variety of Irish dishes, such as ham and cabbage, soda bread, and Irish stew; crafts such as lace and knitting; and an antique show.

Admission: adults, $4; senior citizens, $3; children under 12, free; Friday evening concert, $15.

Location: Festival Hall, Pratt and Sharp streets.

Information: Baltimore Area Visitors Center, (410) 837-4636 or (800) 282-6632.

Tourist Information: Baltimore Area Convention and Visitors Association, (410) 659-7300.

Maryland Wine Festival

Westminster, Md., third weekend in September.

The Carol County Farm Museum is an 1852 farm, with house and outbuildings, surrounded by 140 acres with shade trees, open fields, and a lake. In September, this bucolic location is the site of the Maryland Wine Festival, where a dozen of Maryland's wineries offer tasting and sales. The entrance fee provides 10 tickets for wine tasting, and wine is available for sale by the glass, bottle, and case. The area's restaurants and community groups sell food, and entertainment has included jazz, big-band, and country music. The festival also offers wine-tasting seminars and arts and crafts. It generally runs morning and afternoon on Saturday and through the afternoon on Sunday.

Admission: adults, $10; under 21, free with paying adult.

Location: Carroll County Farm Museum, 500 South Center Street.

Information: Carroll County Farm Museum, (410) 876-2667.

Tourist Information: Carroll County Office of Promotion and Tourism, (410) 848-4500 ext. 2973.

New Market Days
New Market, Md., last full weekend in September.

New Market, the antiques capital of Maryland, recreates a nineteenth-century atmosphere with craftsmen demonstrating
blacksmithing, papermaking, soapmaking, weaving, spinning,
apple-butter making, candlemaking, decoy carving, and chair
caning. Local churches and civic groups provide home-cooked
dishes. Entertainment has included a strolling Dixieland band,
country fiddling, bell-ringing, and country dancing. At Miss Betty's
Colonial Trunk, children experience old-fashioned skills like grinding coffee, writing with quill pens, and striking a flint to make a
fire. Horse-drawn carriages take visitors on rides through the
streets and alleys of New Market. The festival runs mornings and
afternoons on Friday, Saturday, and Sunday.

Admission: free.
Location: Main Street.
Directions: New Market is on Route 144 10 miles west of
   Frederick.
Information: New Market Days Committee, (301) 831-6755.
Tourist Information: Tourism Council of Frederick County,
   Inc., (301) 663-8687.

Oktoberfest
Upper Marlboro, Md., last Sunday in September.

The Washington Saengerbund's Oktoberfest was first held in the
1930s and is considered one of the oldest Oktoberfests in the
country. It is held on the grounds of the German Orphan Home,
which was established by Germans in the 1870s for orphans of
German immigrants. This Oktoberfest is one of the most authentic, with meats and sausages prepared by German butchers, cakes
made by a German bakery according to the Saengerbund's recipes, and imported German beer and wine. Bratwurst, knockwurst,
weisswurst, Kassler rippchen (smoked center-cut pork chops cooked
in beer and sauerkraut), potato salad, soft pretzels, and German

German dancers at the Washington Saengerbund's Oktoberfest.

open-faced sandwiches are some of the foods sold. Through the afternoon and evening, the crowds are entertained beer-hall fashion with two German Oktoberfest bands and performances by German folk dance groups like the Old Washingtonian Schuplattlers.

Admission: $2.

Location: German Orphan Home, Woodyard Road.

Directions: from the Washington Beltway follow Md. Route 4 south for 3 miles; take the Route 223 exit and follow signs 1 mile to the German Orphan Home.

Information: Washington Saengerbund, (301) 251-2883.

Tourist Information: Prince George's County Conference and Visitors Bureau, (301) 967-8687.

New Jersey

New Jersey Ethnic Festival

Jersey City, N.J., third weekend in September.

With the Statue of Liberty, Ellis Island, and the Manhattan skyline as a backdrop, over 200 people are sworn in as U.S. citizens at the New Jersey Ethnic Festival. The opening ceremonies also include a colorful parade of nations, with participating ethnic groups in traditional dress carrying flags and banners. Then, through Saturday and Sunday afternoons, the festival stage features folk songs and dances from around the world. Many of the same groups also sell native foods and handicrafts or exhibit cultural artifacts in Liberty State Park's restored railroad terminal. In addition to the larger ethnic groups, the New Jersey Ethnic Festival includes smaller groups who typically do not hold ethnic festivals of their own. Among them are the Baltic nations, Byelorussians, Slovacs, Hungarians, Belgians, Swedes, and Pakistanis.

Admission: free.
Location: Liberty State Park.
Information: Office of Ethnic Affairs, New Jersey Department of State, (609) 984-7145.
Tourist Information: Gateway Regional Tourism Council, (201) 351-7100.

Wings 'n' Water Festival

Stone Harbor, N.J., third weekend in September.

The Wetlands Institute sponsors the Wings 'n' Water Festival, which celebrates South Jersey's coastal environment. The weekend event has a number of activities focusing on wildlife art, coastal zone protection, and South Jersey culture. Some of the nation's top carvers show their work and participate in the North American Shorebird Carving Championship. Other wildlife artists demonstrate, display, and sell photography, paintings, and sculpture.

The Wings 'n' Water Festival runs morning and afternoon both Saturday and Sunday. Other activities include salt-marsh safaris, back-bay boat cruises, decoy workshops, a regional quilt show, and retriever demonstrations. The U.S. Coast Guard performs air-sea rescues on the beach. Children can enjoy marsh bingo and scavenger hunts. Folk musicians entertain with guitar, Appalachian Mountain dulcimer, and mouth bow and spoons. An old-fashioned seafood dinner—with fresh-caught Jersey flounder, Jersey corn, tomatoes, and coleslaw—is served at Cape May Court House, and booths at nine other locations sell clams on the half shell, shrimp sandwiches, crab-cake sandwiches, Manhattan clam chowder, seafood chowder, seafood salads, and crab fingers.

Admission: adults, $8; children, $2; senior citizens, $6.
Location: Avalon, Stone Harbor, and Cape May Court House.
Directions: from Exit 10 of the Garden State Parkway follow signs to Stone Harbor.
Information: Wetlands Institute, (609) 368-1211.
Tourist Information: Cape May County Chamber of Commerce, (609) 465-7181.

Robert Gibbon Johnson Day Tomato Festival

Salem, N.J., fourth Saturday in September.

On a hot day in July 1820, Colonel Robert Gibbon Johnson stood on the steps of the County Court House in Salem, New Jersey, and did something the people watching him were afraid to do: he ate a tomato. As president of the state agricultural association, Colonel Johnson dramatically demonstrated that the fruit of the tomato, which previously had been cultivated purely as an ornamental plant, was not poisonous, but in fact tasty and refreshing.

Colonel Johnson survived, and today the citizens of Salem celebrate that historic day with a festival. The famous scene, in fact, is reenacted on the Court House steps, and the attending crowd is expected to gasp when the actor playing Colonel Johnson bites into the tomato. The Saturday morning and afternoon festival also features a tomato look-alike contest, a tomato-tossing contest, tomato-recipe judging, musical entertainment, and plenty of foods utilizing the tomato.

Admission: free.

Location: Market Street between Grant Street and Broadway.

Information: Greater Salem Chamber of Commerce, (609) 935-1415.

Garden State Winegrowers Fall Festival

Alternating locations in New Jersey, last weekend in September.

New Jersey's wine industry dates to colonial times, when vintners in the state produced wines for Britain. In 1767, London's Royal Society of Arts recognized two New Jersey vintners for producing America's first high-quality wines. Today New Jersey has 15 wineries, including one of the nation's oldest, founded in 1864. In late September, vintners celebrate the harvest with a fall festival. Held at one of the wineries, the event offers wine tasting and sales, musical entertainment through the afternoon, a variety of foods, arts and crafts, winery tours, hayrides, games, and demonstrations. The festival runs both afternoons, Saturday and Sunday.

Admission: $7.50.

Location: at one of New Jersey's wineries.

Information: New Jersey Wine Industry Advisory Council, (609) 984-9463.

Tourist Information: New Jersey Division of Travel and Tourism, (800) 537-7397.

New York

New York Renaissance Festival

Tuxedo Park, N.Y., weekends from last weekend in July to third weekend in September.

See July—New York.

Capital District Scottish Games

Altamont, N.Y., Saturday of Labor Day weekend.

A highlight of the Capital District Scottish Games is the Northeastern U.S. Pipe Band Championship. In the solo piping contests, pipers play both "light music," such as marches and reels, and "great music"—or in Gaelic, *piobaireachd* (pronounced pee-o-broc)—which consists first of a basic melody followed by increasingly complex variations. Solo pipers are judged on execution, expression, tempo, and tone. Bagpipe bands are similarly rated, but judges also look for a true sound with all bagpipes sounding as one, togetherness in playing, a strong and precise start and finish, and clean transitions between tunes.

The Capital District Scottish Games begin with a Parade of Tartans, a procession of the clans wearing their individual kilts and tartans, followed by the bagpipe bands. There are numerous athletic events, including tossing of the caber, putting of the stone, and tossing the sheaf. At the Northeastern U.S. Open Highland Dance Championship, more than a hundred dancers perform the Seann Truibhas, the Highland Fling, the Sailor's Hornpipe, and the Sword Dance. An exhibition of 14 Scottish breeds of dogs includes a Scottish Dog and Owner Team Contest, where both dress as a famous team like Holmes and Watson or Batman and Robin. The festival also offers entertainment and foods like meat pies, fish and chips, bridies, and shortbreads.

Admission: adults, $8; children ages 6–12, $3; under 6, free.

Location: Altamont Fairgrounds.
Information: Schenectady Pipe Band, (518) 785-5951.
Tourist Information: Albany County Convention and Visitors
    Bureau, (800) 258-3582 or (518) 434-1217.

Golden Harvest Festival

Baldwinsville, N.Y., weekend after Labor Day.

A celebration of autumn, the Golden Harvest Festival has a living
scarecrow contest, where kids dress themselves up with old clothes
stuffed with straw. Others compete to make the best real scarecrow, and a field becomes a gallery for their creations. Young and
old alike can compete to carve the cutest, funniest, and cleverest
animal from a fruit or vegetable, demonstrate their ability at
wild-animal calling, or enter an old-fashioned pie-eating contest.
    Morning and afternoon on Saturday and Sunday, folk musi-
cians play jugs, washtubs, hammered dulcimer, autoharp, fiddle,
and guitar. Over a hundred craftspeople, chosen to appear, show
their work in blacksmithing, basketry, photography, and other
arts. There are puppet shows, storytelling, pony rides, a petting
zoo, and displays of huge vegetables. Local groups sell seasonal
food like fresh pie and hand-pressed cider, along with barbecued
chicken, ribs, meat pies, Cajun potatoes, and corn on the cob.

Admission: adults, $3; children ages 6-17, $1; under 6, free.
Location: Beaver Lake Nature Center.
Directions: from Baldwinsville follow Route 370 west for 2 miles;
    turn right on and follow East Mud Lake Road for 1 mile.
Information: Beaver Lake Nature Center, (315) 638-2519.
Tourist Information: Syracuse-Onondaga Convention and
    Visitors Bureau, (800) 234-4797 or (315) 470-1800.

Feast of San Gennaro

New York, N.Y., two weeks around September 19.

Saint Gennaro, Bishop of Benevento, Italy, led the people of

Naples away from the raging Mount Vesuvius. He died a martyr in 305 A.D. after the Proconsul Timothy had him arrested and tortured. He was first thrown headlong into a furnace, but came through unscathed; then Timothy's agents beheaded him. According to the legend, an old man reverently gathered up Saint Gennaro's body and severed head, and an elderly Neapolitan woman used a sponge to soak up his blood and fill a vial. Neapolitans pray to Saint Gennaro for protection from fires, earthquakes, plagues, droughts, and the eruption of Mount Vesuvius. His solidified blood, kept in the vial, is believed to liquify twice a year, first on the feast of the transfer of his relics, then on September 19, the anniversary of his martyrdom.

Since 1926, Neapolitans in New York's Little Italy have honored Saint Gennaro with a feast in September. For almost two weeks the streets near the Society of San Gennaro are filled with Italian music, carnival games, souvenir booths, and Italian foods. Calzones, macaroni pie, baked ziti, homemade manicotti, scungilli, sausage and peppers, calamari salads, cannoli, noodles in cream, and cheesecake are some of the treats served. The festival runs through the afternoon and evening each day, and the San Gennaro Band performs nightly. On September 19, San Gennaro's Day, a High Mass is held at the Most Precious Blood Church, followed by a procession through the streets of Little Italy.

Admission: free.
Location: Mulberry Street in Little Italy.
Information: San Gennaro Society, (212) 226-9546.
Tourist Information: New York Convention and Visitors Bureau, (212) 397-8222.

Seneca Indian Fall Festival

Irving, N.Y., second weekend in September.

The Seneca tribe celebrates fall with a small festival on the Cattaraugus Indian Reservation in western New York. The festival features Iroquois dancing, crafts, and foods such as corn soup, fried bread, and beans. During the weekend, there are tournaments in softball, football, horseshoes, and lacrosse. There is also a traditional dress competition, a princess pageant, and agricultural and homemaking exhibits. Entertainment has included the Tuscarora Indian Band.

Admission: free.
Location: Route 438, Irving.
Directions: Irving is at Exit 58 off I-90.
Information: Seneca Indian Fall Festival, (716) 532-4900.
Tourist Information: Cattaraugus-Allegany Tourist Bureau, (800) 331-0543 or (716) 938-9111 ext 305.

Festival by the Sea

Hempstead, N.Y., second or third weekend in September.

On the western end of Long Island, Hempstead offers some of Long Island's finer beaches, all within a short drive of Manhattan. The town celebrates its maritime heritage with a weekend festival in September. Each afternoon there is continuous entertainment paired with all sorts of seafood: clams on the half shell, lobster, linguine with clam sauce, and raw oysters. A crafts show includes driftwood sculptures and flower arrangements made with seashells. The festival also includes such things as a surfcasting contest, canoe and sailboat races, sand-sculpture competitions, and air-sea rescue demonstrations.

Admission: free.
Location: Town Park, Lido Beach.
Information: Town Hall, (516) 489-5000.
Tourist Information: Long Island Convention and Visitors Bureau, (800) 441-4601 or (516) 794-4222.

Festival of Grapes

Silver Creek, N.Y., third weekend in September.

Silver Creek lies in one of the country's biggest Concord grape-growing regions, and late in September the village celebrates the grape harvest. There are contests for the best homemade wines, grapevine wreaths, grape desserts, and jams and jellies. Kids can compete at throwing grapes, dressing up their favorite stuffed toy in a grape motif, and grape-bubble-gum blowing. Adults can join the fun at the grape-stomping contest. The festival offers evening concerts, arts and crafts, carnival rides and concessions, and a wine tent, which showcases a local winery and offers wine for sale by the glass, bottle, or case. The Festival of Grapes also includes a waiter and waitress race, Miss Festival of Grapes and Little Miss Festival of Grapes pageants, a classic car show, a bikeathon, and a Grape Bowl high school football game. The festival runs Thursday and Friday evenings and all day Saturday and Sunday.

Admission: free.
Location: village ball park and square.
Information: Festival of Grapes, (716) 366-0547.
Tourist Information: Chautauqua County Vacationlands, (800) 242-4569 or (716) 753-4304.

Naples Grape Festival

Naples, N.Y., third weekend in September.

In the heart of the Finger Lakes wine country in upstate New York, Naples sits amid hills covered with vineyards. The town celebrates the grape harvest in September with two days of arts and crafts, stage entertainment, and foods such as grape pies, grape cakes, and grape tarts. Widmer Wine Cellars offers wine tasting and sales. Entertainment through each afternoon has featured bluegrass, blues, country, and jazz. More than 100 artisans sell their work in wood, leather, glass, pottery, paintings, and fabrics.

Admission: free.
Location: Memorial Town Park.
Information: Naples Grape Festival, P.O. Box 70, Naples, NY 14512.
Tourist Information: Ontario County Four Seasons, (800) 654-9798 or (716) 394-3915.

Atlantic Antic Giant Festival

Brooklyn, N.Y., Sunday in late September.

Held on a 12-block stretch of Atlantic Avenue, the Atlantic Antic Giant Festival is one of Brooklyn's biggest street fairs. The street is lined with hundreds of vendors selling antiques, crafts, and ethnic food, including Chinese, Italian, Polynesian, Swedish, West Indian, Mexican, Arabic, and Cuban dishes. A variety of entertainment is provided on four stages; on the street mimes, strolling musicians, and jugglers wander among the crowds. Reflecting the diversity of the neighborhood, stage performers have included Caribbean dancers, theater groups, jazz ensembles, belly dancers, and steel-drum bands. The festival begins with a colorful parade in the late morning and runs through the afternoon.

Admission: free.
Location: Atlantic Avenue between Fourth Avenue and the East River in Brooklyn Heights.
Information: Atlantic Avenue Committee, (718) 875-8993.
Tourist Information: New York Convention and Visitors Bureau, (212) 397-8222.

Buckwheat Harvest Festival

Penn Yan, N.Y., fourth weekend in September.

The National Buckwheat Institute in Penn Yan serves up "buckwheat everything," including buckwheat fried dough, kasha (buckwheat) crunch ice cream, buckwheat-honey ice cream, buckwheat pizza, and buckwheat shortcake. The musical entertainment through the weekend has included Blood, Sweat and Tears and Sha-Na-Na. Other activities include midway rides, a children's petting zoo, an arts and crafts show, and a Harvest Festival Parade.

Admission: $5.
Location: Festival Grounds, Old Route 14A.
Information: National Buckwheat Institute, (315) 536-7434.

Tourist Information: Finger Lakes Association, (800) 548-4386 or (315) 536-7488.

Remsen Barn Festival of the Arts

Remsen, N.Y., fourth full weekend in September.

The Welsh settlement of Remsen, New York, holds its Barn Festival in the fall. One of the highlights is the *Gymanfa Ganu*, or Welsh hymnfest, with church choirs and soloists performing in two of Remsen's churches on Sunday. On both Saturday and Sunday, Main Street is filled with 250 craft booths offering such things as pottery, quilts, antiques, photography, folk art, and bonsai trees. The festival's Farmers' Market offers locally grown produce, maple products, fudge, and honey. Strolling entertainment has included local barbershop quartets, country-music duos, and folk singers. The festival runs morning and afternoon both days.

Admission: free.
Location: Main Street.
Directions: from Exit 31 of the N.Y. Thruway follow Route 12 north for 15 miles.
Information: Remsen Barn Festival Committee, (315) 831-4257.
Tourist Information: Leatherstocking Country, New York, (800) 233-8778 or (315) 866-1500.

Gore Mountain Region Oktoberfest

North Creek, N.Y., last weekend in September.

At the height of the Adirondack fall foliage colors, Gore Mountain Ski Center in the hamlet of North Creek is the setting for a traditional German Oktoberfest with German food and beer, German folk dancing, and German oompah bands like the Krazy Firemen and the Bavarian Barons. There are also accordion players, yodelers, and men in lederhosen playing the long Alpenhorns. The festival also offers an arts and crafts show, marionettes for the kids, a parade, and gondola rides up Gore Mountain.

Admission: adults, $5; senior citizens and children ages 4–12, $4.
Location: Gore Mountain Ski Center.
Information: Gore Mountain Region Chamber of Commerce, (518) 251-2612.

Pennsylvania

Pennsylvania Renaissance Faire

Manheim, Pa., last weekend in June through second weekend in October.

See June—Pennsylvania.

La Festa Italiana

Scranton, Pa., Labor Day weekend.

Scranton's biggest festival, one of the largest Italian festivals in the area, features three days of entertainment and plenty of Italian food. Around the turn of the century, Italians came to Scranton for coal-mining jobs; their children and grandchildren are among the crowds that attend the event and the performers who appear on stage. Past entertainers have included Italian orchestras, opera singers, ethnic dancers, and nightclub singers from Atlantic City like Julie Dejohn. Vendors lining Court House Square serve Italian dishes and pastries, including ravioli, Italian sausage, pasta fasula, and Italian cookies. The festival runs through the afternoon and evening each of the weekend's three days.

Admission: free.
Location: Court House Square.
Information: La Festa Italiana, (717) 344-7411.
Tourist Information: Greater Scranton Chamber of Commerce, (800) 245-7711 or (717) 342-7711.

National Folk Festival

Johnstown, Pa., Labor Day weekend.

First held in 1934, the National Folk Festival is the first festival to bring folk performers together from a number of ethnic groups and to use the expertise of trained folklorists. Sponsored by the National Council for the Traditional Arts, the National Park Service, and local groups, the festival is held in one city for three years and then moves on to another. Often the city has a history of ethnic diversity, like the steelmaking town of Johnstown, Pennsylvania.

1992 will be the last year the National Folk Festival is in Johnstown, although the local organizers anticipate continuing with a folk festival of their own. In Johnstown, the festival has included dancers from the Ukraine, a throat singer from Mongolia, a Louisiana zydeco band, a Piedmont blues singer, the Missouri Fiddlers, the Cherokee Indian Baptist Choir, and a singer of Balkan Sephardic music. The musicians perform continuously on four stages through most of the weekend. The festival also includes craftspeople making such things as Polish paper-cutting pieces, Mexican piñatas, and Irish lace. Local community groups sell ethnic food. The festival runs Friday evening, Saturday afternoon and evening, and Sunday afternoon.

Admission: free.

Location: Cambria City neighborhood at Broad Street.

Information: Johnstown Area Heritage Association, (814) 539-1889.

Tourist Information: Altoona-Blair Convention and Visitors Bureau, (814) 943-4183.

Polish-American Festival

Doylestown, Pa., Labor Day weekend and the following weekend.

The National Shrine of Our Lady of Czestochowa (pronounced chen-sto-hova) is the American counterpart of a shrine in Poland that holds an ancient painting of the Holy Mother and the Christ

Child. According to tradition, St. Luke the Evangelist painted the picture on wood from a table in the Holy Family's home. Since 1382, the Pauline Fathers have protected the painting in its shrine in Czestochowa, Poland, and in the 1950s they established the American shrine at Doylestown. It holds a faithful reproduction of the painting, which is an object of veneration for American pilgrims.

Soon after the Feast of Our Lady of Czestochowa on August 26, the Polish-American Festival is held on the grounds of the National Shrine. Each day of Labor Day weekend and the following weekend is filled with Polish music and dance on four stages. Polish dishes served include plaskie (potato pancakes), pierogi (dumplings stuffed with sauerkraut, potatoes, cheese, or prune filling), and golambki (stuffed cabbage). In a recreated Polish village there are demonstrations of wood carving, pisanki (egg coloring), making babka (or grandmothers') bread, grinding horseradish, and shredding and packing sauerkraut. The festival also includes carnival rides, a bike race, a foot race, and the National Kielbasa Cook-off.

Admission: $4.

Location: National Shrine of Our Lady of Czestochowa, Ferry Road.

Information: National Shrine of Our Lady of Czestochowa, (215) 345-0600.

Tourist Information: Bucks County Tourist Commission, (215) 345-4552.

Farmers' and Threshermen's Jubilee

New Centerville, Pa., weekend following Labor Day.

In the Laurel Highlands of western Pennsylvania, the citizens of the small town of New Centerville have been celebrating harvest time since 1953 with the Farmers' and Threshermen's Jubilee. The event is also known for the antique farm equipment displayed and demonstrated, which has included a ground-hog thresher, a dog-powered butter churn, and hit-and-miss gas engines.

The Jubilee is a rural festival, with tractor-pulling competitions, outhouse-on-wheels races, log-chopping contests, and a quilt show and sale. The festival runs nearly all day from Wednesday through Sunday, and entertainment is provided afternoons and evenings. Past acts have included the Blue Mountain Cloggers, Yodeling Al and Jean Shade, and the Sandspring Bluegrass Band. There is a hoedown square dance on Saturday night. Home-style food is plentiful, including a chicken barbecue Friday, Saturday, and Sunday afternoons.

Admission: adults, $3; senior citizens (over 65), $2; children under 14, free.

Location: Jubilee Grounds.

Directions: nine miles south of Somerset, Pa., on Route 281.

Information: Farmers' and Threshermen's Jubilee, (814) 926-3142.

Tourist Information: Laurel Highlands, Inc., (800) 333-5661 or (412) 238-5661.

Ligonier Highland Games

Ligonier, Pa., first Saturday after Labor Day.

One of the events at the Ligonier Highland Games is the tossing of the caber, where brawny athletes in kilts throw a 100- to 130-pound, 17- to 21-foot pole end over end so that the small end of the caber points directly away from the contestant. The athlete with the straightest toss is the winner. Another event, the tossing of the sheaf, involves pitching a bale of hay over a bar. In the Scottish hammer throw, contestants try to throw a 16- to 22-pound long-handled hammer the longest distance.

Besides the Scottish games, this festival offers music and dance, including performances on the Celtic harp, bell ringing, Scottish fiddling, and Scottish country dancing. There are competitions in Scottish dancing, piping, and drumming; children's games; border-collie sheep-herding demonstrations; rugby; and massed pipe band performances. Booths are set up for the various clans, and vendors sell woolens, shortbreads, and meat pies.

Admission: adults, $8; children ages 6–12, $4; under 6, free.

Making bean soup at the McClure Bean Soup Festival.

Location: Idlewild Park, 3 miles west of Ligonier on U.S. Route 30.

Information: Idlewild Park, (412) 238-3666.

Tourist Information: Laurel Highlands, Inc., (800) 333-5661 or (412) 238-5661.

McClure Bean Soup Festival

McClure, Pa., second week in September.

Civil War veterans started meeting in McClure, a town in central Pennsylvania, in 1883 to trade war stories and eat the bean soup they had known in the field. In 1891, organizers of the event began allowing the general public to attend and taste some real Civil War bean soup. Comrade Ner B. Middleswarth, the chairman in charge, even persuaded the War Department to furnish hard tack for the occasion.

Today, bean soup of the original recipe (hamburger, beans, and lard) is still cooked over wood fires in big cast-iron kettles. A group of men—some wearing Civil War uniforms—work in a section of a large white pavilion, stirring sixteen 35-gallon kettles of soup. When a kettle of soup is ready, a pulley carries the entire kettle to a serving counter. People eat the bean soup family-style at long tables in the pavilion.

The McClure Bean Soup Festival runs Tuesday, Wednesday, and Thursday evening and all day Friday and Saturday. The organizers have added entertainment, political speeches, carnival rides, games, and concession food, but the bean soup dinners remain much the same as Civil War families enjoyed a century ago.

Admission: free.

Location: Cold Springs Grove on Ohio Street.

Information: McClure Bean Soup Association, (717) 658-8425.

Tourist Information: Susquehanna Valley Visitors Bureau, (800) 458-4748 or (717) 743-7234.

Chester County Restaurant Festival

West Chester, Pa., Sunday in mid-September.

Strawberry pie, appetizers made with Chester County mushrooms, shrimp stuffed with crab imperial, gyros, souvlakia, veal scaloppine, Cajun chicken grill, pork lo mein, and chicken in orange brandy sauce are some of the treats offered at the Chester County Restaurant Festival. Over 30 chefs from the area's most popular restaurants offer their favorite dishes at booths set up on Market Street in historic West Chester. Festival visitors can enjoy the food while listening to live music or wandering the town's cobblestone streets. Sponsored by the Brandywine Restaurant Association, the festival benefits the association's scholarship fund.

Admission: free.

Location: Market Street.

Information: Chester County Tourist Bureau, (800) 228-9933 or (215) 344-6365.

Pennsylvania Bow Hunters Festival

Forksville, Pa., third weekend in September.

Some of the best archers in the country attend and demonstrate their skills at the Pennsylvania Bow Hunters Festival. Stacy Groscup, a well-known instinctive archer, can hit an aspirin tablet thrown in the air at 30 feet. Olympic gold medalists and world champions have also attended.

Held just before archery season, the Bow Hunters Festival draws some 3,000 archers to practice and demonstrate their skill at hitting moving and stationary targets. The event also features a Saturday evening bluegrass concert, archery clinics, exhibits, competitions, and concessions. The festival runs morning and afternoon Friday through Sunday.

Admission: $2.
Location: Forksville Fairgrounds.
Directions: from Dushore follow Pa. Route 87 south for 12 miles.
Information: Pennsylvania Bow Hunters Festival, (717) 525-3635.
Tourist Information: Endless Mountains Visitors Bureau, (717) 836-5431.

Covered Bridge Festival

Washington and Greene counties, Pa., third weekend in September.

Washington and Greene counties have 35 covered bridges, and eight of them serve as the sites of a festival in late September. The entertainment and food provided at each bridge varies, but much of it is homespun and rural. Among the foods are barbecued chicken, Belgian sausage, corn on the cob, sweet sausage, elephant ears, cabbage and noodles, ham barbecue, sauerkraut and kielbasa, and homemade pies. Entertainment has included magic shows, storytelling, square dancing, old-time fiddling, barbershop quartets, the Ukrainian Dance Troop, and Kitch's Steam Calliope. Each bridge offers arts and crafts, and some provide a

children's area. Often local clubs sponsor antique equipment demonstrations, reenactments, and historical displays. The Covered
Bridge Festival runs Saturday morning and afternoon and Sunday afternoon.

Admission: free.
Location: eight different covered bridges in Washington and
Greene counties.
Information: Washington County Tourism, (412) 222-8130.

Little Buffalo Festival of the Arts
Newport, Pa., third weekend in September.

This rural county and the small Little Buffalo State Park host an
impressive arts festival with around 100 performers and a juried
arts and crafts show. The show draws artists from far and wide
and includes folk art, handwoven clothing, photography, and
paintings. A wide variety of music and entertainment—ranging
from choral music to salsa, from folk to Broadway—appears on
four stages. While many of the performers are local, a few outside
groups are included. One year Amigo, a 20-piece musical group
from Mexico City, performed. The festival, which runs Saturday
and Sunday afternoons, also offers a children's creative area and
food concessions.

Admission: adults, $4.00; children 11 and under, $2.00.
Location: Little Buffalo State Park.
Information: Perry County Council of the Arts, (717) 567-7023.
Tourist Information: Perry County Tourist and Recreation
Bureau, (717) 834-4912.

Penn's Colony Festival
Prospect, Pa., last two weekends in September.

The Penn's Colony Festival re-creates a colonial settlement, with
authentically costumed craftspeople and artisans selling their
work in an outdoor marketplace. Colonial military and Indian

encampments and reenactments, artillery demonstrations, and performances by fife and drum corps, Irish dancers, and theater groups add to the festivities. Craftspeople offer such things as leather goods, wickerwork, pottery, dolls, stained glass, and fine furniture. Children can participate in sack races, tug-o'-war, and nine-pins. Food includes colonial soups, roast pork, apple fritters, and pioneer pastries. The festival runs mornings and afternoons on Saturday and Sunday of both weekends.

Admission: adults, $3.50; senior citizens, $3; children ages 6-16, $2.50; group rates available.

Location: Camp Lutherlyn.

Directions: from intersection of U.S. Route 422 and Route 528 follow Route 528 south for 1 mile.

Information: Penn's Colony Association, (412) 241-8006.

Tourist Information: The Magic Forests of West Central Pennsylvania, (800) 348-9393 or (814) 849-5197.

Mt. Pleasant Glass Festival

Mt. Pleasant, Pa., weekend in late September.

Glass is Mt. Pleasant's major industry, and the town celebrates the glass industry in September with three days of music, food, rides, and contests. Mt. Pleasant's three glass companies—Lenox Crystal, L. E. Smith Glass, and Electro-Glass—set up exhibits on Washington Street and offer demonstrations of glassblowing and cutting. Through the weekend, continuous entertainment is scheduled on two stages, and evening concerts Friday and Saturday feature well-known artists. Music ranges from country singers to polka bands to gospel choruses.

One of the highlights of the festival is the twins contest on Sunday. Following rules established in Twinsburg, Ohio, twins are judged in 10 categories, including most identical, least identical, and most talented. About 100 sets of twins attend, ranging in age from 8 months to 80 years. The festival also includes a Kidsfest, with T-shirt painting, pie-eating contests, and other fun activities for children under 12. There are also glass artists, Miss Glass Festival and Little Miss Glass Festival contests, a parade, and 20 booths of ethnic and festival food. The festival runs through the afternoon and evening on Friday, Saturday, and Sunday.

Admission: free.
Location: Washington Street.
Information: Mt. Pleasant Glass Festival, (412) 547-6745.
Tourist Information: Laurel Highlands, Inc., (800) 333-5661 or (412) 238-5661.

Chevrolet Celtic Classic Highland Games and Festival

Bethlehem, Pa., last weekend in September.

Celebrating Irish, Scottish, and Welsh cultures, the Celtic Classic features Highland games, dancing competitions, and music of the British Isles. Irish stew, Cornish pasties, bridies, scones, shortbread, fish and chips, and toad-in-the-hole are some of the ethnic specialties served at the festival.

The Celtic Classic begins on Friday evening with musical entertainment. Saturday and Sunday are filled with competitions—the Highland games athletic competition, a bagpipe bands competition, a classical *piobaireachd* bagpiping competition, and a Celtic dancing competition. Each day there is a featured concert of music from the British Isles, children's entertainment, and sales of Celtic wares.

Admission: free.
Location: downtown Bethlehem.
Information: Chevrolet Celtic Classic, (215) 868-9599.
Tourist Information: Lehigh Convention and Visitors Bureau, Inc., (800) 747-0561 or (215) 266-0560.

Wine Country Harvest Festival

North East, Pa., fourth weekend in September.

The low hills rising from the shores of Lake Erie have proved ideal for the culture of grapes. In the 1850s, William Griffith planted three acres of grapes; today there are 13,000 acres of vineyards, the annual harvest amounts to about 80,000 tons, and the area is one of the largest Concord grape-growing regions in the world. It also grows other varieties, including Catawba, Niagara, Delaware, and Cayuga White, as well as European grapes such as Chardonnay, White Riesling, and Pinot Noir. The area is Pennsylvania's chief wine-growing region, with four major wineries.

Each year the town of North East celebrates the grape harvest with a festival under century-old trees in Gibson Park. There is, of course, plenty of grape treats, including freshly picked bunches, sparkling grape juice, grape ice cream, homemade grape pies, and jams and jellies. A wine tent sells selections from the area's wineries by the glass, and shuttle buses travel to the wineries for tasting and tours. The festival's main stage offers entertainment through the weekend, including blues, bluegrass, barbershop, rock and roll, country, and big-band music, and a street dance is held Saturday night. The festival also includes arts and crafts, grape-stomping contests, bed races, a vineyards bicycle tour, and a farmers' market. The festival runs from Friday evening until Sunday evening.

Admission: free.
Location: Gibson Park.
Information: North East Chamber of Commerce, (814) 725-4262.
Tourist Information: Tourist and Convention Bureau of Erie County, (814) 454-7191.

Virginia

International Children's Festival

Vienna, Va., Labor Day weekend.

Although oriented to children, people of all ages enjoy the music, dance, and art presented at the International Children's Festival. Each year performers—many of them children themselves—come

Juggler entertains a crowd at the International Children's Festival.

from around the world and across the country to Wolftrap, America's only national park devoted solely to the arts. One returning favorite is Halau Hula Olana, a hula dance troupe from Hawaii with 30 boys and girls between the ages of 7 and 14. The Chinese Youth Folk Sports of Taiwan demonstrate their adeptness with diabolo spinning, shuttlecock kicking, and rope jumping. The National Symphonic Youth Band of Costa Rica has also appeared at the festival.

The International Children's Festival runs morning through afternoon each day, Saturday through Monday of Labor Day Weekend. Five stages feature continuous performances by dance groups, folk singers, acrobats, cloggers, magicians, storytellers, mimes, jugglers, and puppeteers. Children can also participate in hands-on workshops where they learn such things as weaving, brass rubbing, paper-flowermaking, Chinese stencils, and how to make Indonesian hand puppets. Over 35,000 people attend the festival, which is sponsored by the Fairfax County Council of the Arts in cooperation with the National Park Service.

Admission: adults, $8; senior citizens, $6; children ages 3–12, $6; children under 3, free.
Location: Wolf Trap Farm Park for the Performing Arts.
Directions: from Capital Beltway take Dulles Toll Road to Wolf Trap Exit.
Information: Fairfax County Council of the Arts, (703) 642-0862.
Tourist Information: Fairfax County Tourism and Convention Bureau, (703) 790-3329.

Dock Boggs Festival

Wise, Va., second Saturday in September.

Moran Lee "Dock" Boggs was a coal miner, traditional music composer, and banjo player in Wise, Virginia. The Dock Boggs festival of traditional music honors him as well as Kate Peters Sturgill, another Wise County musician and composer. The day is filled with performances of traditional mountain music; most of the musicians are from southwestern Virginia or nearby Kentucky and Tennessee. Appalachian mountain foods like soup beans, cornbread, fried potatoes, greens, fried pies, and molasses stack cakes are served. There are demonstrations of apple-buttermaking in an open kettle, churning fresh milk into butter, grinding corn into cornmeal, lye-soapmaking, and cidermaking. Craftspeople sell quilts, crochet work, woodwork, and needlepoint.

Admission: adults, $3; children under 12, $2.
Location: Wise County Fairgrounds.
Information: Clinch Valley College, (703) 328-0100.
Tourist Information: Southwest Blue Ridge Highlands, Inc., (703) 431-4300.

Hampton Bay Days

Hampton, Va., second full weekend in September.

Hampton, a port on the Chesapeake Bay, celebrates its maritime heritage with a three-day festival. One highlight of the event is the top-name entertainment, which has included the Beach Boys, Bruce Hornsby and the Range, Tammy Wynette, The Hooters, George Jones, and Eddie Rabbitt. Four stages offer continuous performances by both national and local entertainers through the weekend. The festival also includes athletic events, a juried fine art exhibit, an arts and crafts show, water-skiing shows, tall ships, a raft race, and Chesapeake Bay education and awareness exhibits. Vendors sell all kinds of seafood, including crab, shrimp, and flounder. More than 200,000 people attend Hampton Bay Days, which runs from Friday noon to Sunday evening.

Admission: free.

Location: on the waterfront.

Information: Hampton Visitor Center, (800) 487-8778.

Tourist Information: Hampton Department of Conventions and Tourism, (804) 722-1222.

Mathews Market Days

Mathews, Va., weekend following Labor Day.

The village of Mathews sits in Tidewater Virginia on the Chesapeake Bay, where fishing is a major industry. The village was made a county seat 200 years ago, and the quaint courthouse was completed in 1793. Here, on the Court House Green, the people of Mathews hold a community festival with entertainment, arts and crafts, and food. There is plenty of fresh, local seafood, including crab cakes, crab salad, crab muffins, and crab fritters. Most of the activities are on Saturday, including performances by local musicians, a watermelon-seed spitting contest, the Governor's Cup Blue Crab Derby (a crab race), and a Saturday evening street dance.

Admission: free.

Location: Court House Green, in the center of town.

Information: Mathews Cooperative Extension Service, (804) 725-7196.

Tourist Information: Mathews County Chamber of Commerce, (804) 725-9029.

Rockbridge Mountain Music and Dance Convention

Buena Vista, Va., second weekend after Labor Day.

The Rockbridge Mountain Music and Dance Convention is a small, informal two-day festival of old-time mountain music, the vocal and string music that preceded bluegrass and country-and-western music. No performances are scheduled; instead the stage is open Friday evening and Saturday afternoon for musicians, singers, and dancers who wish to perform, and both locals and better-known musicians appear. One of the festival's founders and sometime performer is the brother of folk singer Pete Seeger, Mike Seeger, who has an international reputation and more than 50 records of traditional music and his own compositions. The festival also presents a Saturday-night southern-style square and round dance, with a local caller and band. A natural-foods store sells health foods during the festival, and a pancake breakfast is often held Saturday morning. Many of the festivalgoers camp at the park, and jam sessions around campfires stretch into the night.

Admission: $5.
Location: Glen Maury Park.
Directions: from Buena Vista follow Route 501 south for 1.5 miles, then turn right onto 10th Street to park.
Information: Glen Maury Park, (703) 261-7321.
Tourist Information: Buena Vista Chamber of Commerce, (703) 261-2880.

International Food Festival

Richmond, Va., weekend in the middle of September.

Danish vafler (lace waffles), Filipino pancit (stir-fried meat, seafood, rice noodles, and vegetables), Greek spanacopeta (spinach turnovers), Lithuanian grybai (mushroom cookies), and Vietnamese thit bo nuong (beef on a stick) are some of the foods served at Richmond's International Food Festival, Virginia's largest multicultural event. Representatives from more than 30 nationalities and American regional groups serve authentic foods at booths throughout Richmond's convention center. Through the weekend, the festival's stage features folk music, dancing, and pageants. The festival also offers an international bazaar, heritage exhibits, a Sweets Street, and children's programs. The International Food Festival generally runs Friday evening and Saturday and Sunday afternoon and evening.

Admission: $4; in advance, $3; children under 6, free.
Location: Richmond Centre.
Information: The Boys Clubs of Richmond, Inc., (804) 353-4389.
Tourist Information: Metro Richmond Convention and Visitors Bureau, (804) 782-2777.

Virginia Beach Neptune Festival

Virginia Beach, Va., last two weeks of September.

The resort city of Virginia Beach ends its summer season with a bang. The 16-day Neptune Festival attracts nearly one million people and offers a variety of activities, including a surfing classic, a country-fair day, an arts and crafts show, a grand parade, and a rousing fireworks display. One popular event is the sandcastle competition, with competitors ranging from schoolchildren to local architectural and engineering firms.

Although activities are planned through the festival's two weeks, the last weekend is when the streets and boardwalk really come to life. Five stages offer entertainment from karate demonstrations to country-and-western performances. The surfing classic and the sandcastle competition run through the weekend, and there are special events, like an air show by the U.S. Navy Blue Angels. One downtown street is turned into a Medieval Street Faire, while another location is the center of a Hellenic Festival.

Each year, an outstanding citizen of Virginia Beach is chosen to reign as King Neptune. His court includes several Royal Ladies of the Realm plus six princesses selected from the city's high schools. The princesses and ladies are escorted by Neptune's Tritons, some of the city's business leaders. Together, King Neptune and his court reign over the festival.

Admission: free.
Location: citywide and on the boardwalk for the last weekend.
Information: Virginia Beach Events Unlimited, Inc., (804) 498-0215.
Tourist Information: Virginia Beach Department of Convention and Visitor Development, (804) 437-4700.

Edinburg Ole Time Festival

Edinburg, Va., third full weekend in September.

On Thompson's Porch, an eight-woman band called the Kitchen Klankers play drums made from food cans and a plastic wastebasket, a washboard and thimbles, a bass fiddle made from a bucket with a cord connecting a mop, and jugs and kazoos. Entertainment at the Edinburg Ole Time Festival also has included the Country Western Dancers, bluegrass bands, cloggers, and accordion player Bill McElroy. Country dances are usually held Friday and Saturday nights. Several churches hold gospel and hymn sings and Civil War groups reenact a Blue-and-Gray battle. Throughout the festival local groups serve barbecued chicken, ham potpie, old-fashioned dinners, and country breakfasts. The festival generally runs Friday evening, all day Saturday, and Sunday morning and afternoon. Most activities are on Saturday.

Admission: free.
Location: Main Street and Stoney Creek Boulevard.
Information: Edinburg Area Chamber of Commerce, (703) 984-8521.
Tourist Information: Shenandoah County Economic Development Council, (703) 459-5522.

Poquoson Seafood Festival

Poquoson, Va., third weekend in September.

Poquoson sits on the Chesapeake Bay not far from where the bay joins the Atlantic Ocean. For three days the Poquoson Seafood Festival offers some savory dishes from the surrounding waters, including crab cakes, shrimp, scallops, and chowder. The good food is accompanied by local musical entertainment such as the Boneshakers, Slapwater, Fat Ammon's Band, and the Janitors. The festival also offers an arts and crafts show, a 5-kilometer run, a parade, a Saturday-night fireworks display, and the Poquoson Workboat Race. The festival runs Friday evening, all day Saturday, and Sunday afternoon.

Admission: free.
Location: Poquoson City Park.
Information: Poquoson Parks and Recreation, (804) 868-9745.
Tourist Information: Virginia Peninsula Tourist Information Center, (804) 886-2737.

Grayson Highlands Fall Festival

Mouth of Wilson, Va., last full weekend in September.

Grayson Highlands State Park sits high in the Appalachian Mountains of southwestern Virginia, not far from Virginia's highest point, Mount Rogers. In late September when the leaves are beginning to turn, the park is the setting for a small festival, with two afternoons of bluegrass, gospel, and old-time music. Appalachian craftspeople sell such things as black-powder muskets, quilts, wooden furniture, pottery, and baskets. On Saturday afternoon the Pony Association auctions off some of the ponies that roam wild through the park. The festival also offers barbecued chicken dinners and demonstrations on how to make apple butter, molasses, and cider.

Admission: $2.
Location: Grayson Highlands State Park.
Directions: from Galax, follow U.S. Route 58 west for 40 miles.
Information: Grayson Highlands State Park, (703) 579-7092.
Tourist Information: Southwest Blue Ridge Highlands, Inc., (703) 431-4300.

West Virginia

Charleston Sternwheel Regatta

Charleston, W.Va., nine days preceding Labor Day.

See August—West Virginia.

Hick Festival

Parsons, W.Va., Labor Day weekend.

For more than 20 years, the Hick Festival has celebrated the colorful logging history of the village of Hendricks. Contests include woodchopping, crosscut sawing, tobacco spitting, ax throwing, horse pulling, banjo and fiddle playing, horseshoe pitching, and arm wrestling. Country and bluegrass entertainment, gospel sings, a queen's coronation and parade, a horse show, local crafts, and a coon chase are also featured. Open-pit beef and barbecue dinners are served. The festival usually runs afternoons and evenings on Saturday and Sunday and morning and afternoon on Labor Day.

Admission: free.
Location: Camp Kidd Park.
Information: Hendrick's Ruritan Club, Route 2, Box 46, Parsons, WV 26287.
Tourist Information: Tucker County Convention and Visitors Bureau, (800) 782-2775 or (304) 259-5315.

Stonewall Jackson Heritage Arts and Crafts Jubilee

Weston, W.Va., Labor Day weekend.

Jackson's Mill, the boyhood home of General T. J. "Stonewall" Jackson, is the setting for a celebration of the rich heritage of the West Virginia hills. Over a hundred craftspeople—potters, woodworkers, weavers, glassblowers, and others—demonstrate, exhibit, and sell their work, all made from natural materials. Special quilt, art, needle art, and photo shows exhibit the work of talented West Virginians. Musical performances through the four-day festival feature traditional Appalachian music and the sounds of fiddle, banjo, and dulcimer. The festival also offers Civil War encampments, a turkey-calling contest, the West Virginia State Pie Baking Contest, and an antique engine show. Country meals include corn bread and beans, pancakes and sausage, and barbecued chicken.

Admission: adults, $4; senior citizens, $3; children under 12, $1.

Location: Jackson's Mill 4-H Conference Center.

Directions: from Weston exit off I-79 follow Route 33 to Weston, then follow Route 19 north to Jackson's Mill Road.

Information: Stonewall Jackson Heritage Arts and Crafts Jubilee, (304) 269-1863.

Tourist Information: Lewis County Convention and Visitors Bureau, (304) 269-7328.

West Virginia Italian Heritage Festival

Clarksburg, W.Va., Labor Day weekend.

The West Virginia Italian Heritage Festival kicks off Friday at noon with the coronation of Regina Maria, the festival queen. Through the rest of the day and all day Saturday and Sunday, two stages on Main Street provide continuous entertainment. Headliner performers in past years have included Jerry Vale, Al Martino, Frankie Avalon, the Gaylords, and Maria Muldaur, but much of the entertainment is Italian, such as I'Campagnoli, Figli Del Sole, and various Italian folk dance groups, orchestras, and singers.

The festival's cultural program offers an Italian film festival, opera, ballet, poetry readings, and an art show featuring Italian artists. There are morra and boccie tournaments and a homemade wine contest. Italian food booths serve pasta, Italian sausage, fish dishes, and desserts, and Italian wine is served in the Wine Garden. Other activities during the weekend include a Saturday morning parade, an outdoor Sunday Mass, and street dancing.

Admission: free.
Location: Main Street.
Information: West Virginia Italian Heritage Festival, Inc., (304) 622-7314.
Tourist Information: Clarksburg Convention and Visitors Bureau, (304) 622-9199.

Treasure Mountain Festival

Franklin, W.Va., third weekend in September.

In 1758 a band of Shawnee Indians raided and looted Fort Seybert, leaving with prisoners and a kettle full of the fort's valuables. On the escape route to the Ohio River Valley, the heavy kettle was buried and the Indians continued on, never to return for the loot. Franklin celebrates the Treasure Mountain legend with a Mountain Man and Woman Contest, muzzleloader competitions, a beard and mustache contest, a fiddlers' contest, a banjo contest, a horseshoe tournament, storytelling, historical dramas, a period-costumes competition, and the Treasure Mountain Parade. The festival also offers street dances, gospel singers, and country music performances. Among the country foods served are pancakes and sausage, lamb barbecue, and country ham potpie. The festival runs all day Friday and Saturday and through the morning and afternoon on Sunday.

Admission: free.
Location: Main Street and Town Park.
Information: Treasure Mountain Festival Association, (304) 249-5422.
Tourist Information: Potomac Highlands Convention and Visitors Bureau, (304) 636-8400.

Mason-Dixon Festival

Morgantown, W.Va., weekend in late September.

Held on the shores of the Monongahela River, the Mason-Dixon Festival celebrates Morgantown's river heritage. From Friday

evening until Sunday evening, the festival offers country music
and folk dancing. Past performers have included the Fabulous
Twister Sisters, Stewed Mulligan, and dulcimer player Wurley
Gardener. River activities include sternwheeler races, water-skiing shows, boat parades, a collegiate rowing regatta, and historical cruises.

Admission: free.
Location: Morgantown Riverfront Park.
Information: Mason-Dixon Festival, (304) 599-1104.
Tourist Information: Northern West Virginia Convention and
   Visitors Bureau, (800) 458-7373 or (304) 292-5081.

Mountaineer Balloon Festival

Morgantown, W.Va., weekend in late September or October.

Scores of hot-air balloons, each a different design and color, quietly rise above the West Virginia mountains during the morning
and evening launches. The Mountaineer Balloon Festival also
features nighttime launches, when the balloons' propane burners
give them the appearance of giant floating lanterns. During the
day, visitors can take tethered balloon rides or enjoy aerobatic
shows, musical entertainment, amusement rides, lacrosse scrim-
mages, antique car shows, arts and crafts, and festival food. The
festival generally runs Thursday and Friday evenings and all day
Saturday and Sunday, with most activities scheduled for the
weekend afternoons.

Admission: adults, $3; teens, $2; children, $1; preschoolers, free;
   per carload, $10.
Location: Morgantown Airport, Hart Field.
Directions: Follow U.S. Route 48 to Pierpont Road Exit 7; follow
   Route 857 south to Route 119 north; look for festival or airport
   signs.
Information: BOPARC, (304) 296-8356.
Tourist Information: Northern West Virginia Convention and
   Visitors Bureau, (800) 458-7373 or (304) 292-5081.

Preston County Buckwheat Festival

Kingwood, W.Va., four days beginning last Thursday of September.

The Kingwood Volunteer Fire Department serves buckwheat cake and sausage meals morning until night each day of the Preston County Buckwheat Festival. First held in 1938, the festival attracts 100,000 people; they can enjoy the coronation of Queen Ceres and King Buckwheat, three parades, a Banjo and Fiddlers' Contest, a swine showmanship contest, an antique car show, and a turkey-calling contest. The Country Music Spectacular, usually held Friday evening, has featured top performers like the Charlie Daniels Band and Barbara Mandrell. The festival generally runs all day Thursday, Friday, and Saturday, and morning and afternoon on Sunday.

Admission: free.

Location: Brown Avenue and Price Street.

Information: Kingwood Volunteer Fire Department, P.O. Box 74, Kingwood, WV 26537.

Tourist Information: Preston County Chamber of Commerce, (304) 329-0576.

October

Maryland

Maryland Renaissance Festival

Annapolis, Md., weekends from last weekend in August to second weekend in October.

See August—Maryland.

Fell's Point Fun Festival

Baltimore, Md., first full weekend in October.

In the 1960s, the preservation society of Fell's Point started this festival to pay off the debt incurred in saving the quaint historic neighborhood from two interstate highways. Today the debt is paid, and the Fell's Point Fun Festival has become Baltimore's biggest street festival. Fell's Point remains one of Baltimore's most interesting neighborhoods, with a pleasant waterfront, colonial and Victorian town houses, and narrow cobblestone streets.

Over 200,000 people pack the streets to enjoy continuous entertainment on four stages, visit the 200 crafts booths, and eat festival foods like steamed crabs, pit-cooked beef, and french fries. Musical entertainment runs from classic rock to rhythm and blues to German brass bands. At the Family and Children's Center, kids can make their own scarecrow, jump around in the Moon Bounce, or go for a pony ride. The festival runs afternoons and evenings Saturday and Sunday.

Ring jousting at the Maryland State Jousting Championship and Horse Festival.

Admission: $1.
Location: Fell's Point at Broadway and Thames streets.
Information: Fell's Point Fun Festival, (410) 675-6756.
Tourist Information: Baltimore Area Convention and Visitors
    Association, (410) 659-7300.

Maryland State Jousting Championship and Horse Festival

Bel Air, Md., first Sunday in October.

Jousting is Maryland's state sport, and on a Sunday in October
jousters from all over the state come to the Harford County

Equestrian Center to compete for the state championship. In modern jousting, horsemen race down an 80-yard course holding a lance that looks like a broomstick with a darning needle on the end of it. After a 20-yard start, they encounter three arches spaced 30 yards apart, each with a ring hung at horse's height from a cord. The rings range in diameter from 1 3/4 inches down to 1/4 inch. Jousters must race down the course in less than nine seconds and catch the rings on the lance.

Jousting competitions are held all day, with the championship starting in midafternoon. Through the day, the festival offers a miniature-horse show, a plantation walking-horse exhibit, and vaulting demonstrations. The Marklind Medieval Militia puts on a mock medieval battle, and the Maryland State Jousting Association stages a medieval joust and a Rings of Fire joust where the jousting rings are set on fire. A parade precedes the championship, and bagpipe bands, medieval jesters, and equestrian marching units perform during the day.

Admission: adults, $3; children ages 7–12, $1; under 7, free.

Location: Harford County Equestrian Center, 700 North Tollgate Road.

Information: Harford County Tourism and Promotion Division, (410) 838-6000, ext. 339.

Autumn Glory Festival

Oakland, Md., second full weekend in October.

The Appalachian Mountains in western Maryland turn to bright reds, oranges, and yellows in the middle of October, when Garrett County holds its Autumn Glory Festival. During the four days of the festival there are many events, but the most interesting include the Maryland State Five-String Banjo Championship, the Maryland State Fiddle Championship, the Western Maryland Tournament of Bands, and the Grand Feature Parade. There are also bagpipe band concerts, western-style square dancing, arts and crafts, and an antique show. Garrett County turkey dinners are held throughout the festival.

Admission: free; charges for some events.

Location: various locations in Oakland and in Garrett County.
Information: Deep Creek Lake-Garrett County Promotion
Council, (301) 334-1948.

Catoctin Colorfest

Thurmont, Md., second weekend in October.

When Maryland's Catoctin Mountains are ablaze in fall colors,
communities nearby celebrate with an October weekend festival.
The event has been held for about 30 years and now attracts
100,000 people. The center of the festival is Thurmont's Community Park, which through the weekend offers more than a hundred arts and crafts booths, pancake and sausage breakfasts,
fried chicken dinners, and local entertainment. Several hundred
other artisans exhibit their work at other locations. Churches, fire
companies, and local clubs serve fried oyster dinners, crab soup,
country ham sandwiches, chicken corn soup, and chicken potpie
dinners. The festival also offers apple-butter boiling, Civil War
reenactments, sheep-shearing demonstrations, petting zoos, antique automobile shows, and gospel music singing.

Admission: free.
Location: various locations in Thurmont and nearby communities.
Information: Catoctin Colorfest, Inc., (301) 271-4432.
Tourist Information: Tourism Council of Frederick County,
(301) 663-8687.

Patuxent River Appreciation Days

Solomons, Md., second weekend in October.

Celebrating Maryland's largest in-state river, the Patuxent River
Appreciation Days takes place at Solomons, where the river flows
into the Chesapeake Bay. Three boats—a restored 1899 buy boat,
a large charter fishing boat, and a workboat—cruise Solomons
Harbor, offering free rides. At the Calvert Marine Museum, entertainment has included folk musicians singing sea chanteys, a
local gospel choir, and a string band. Children can enjoy puppet

Jazz musicians at the St. Mary's County Oyster Festival.

shows, make their own toy sailboat, or learn about marine life of the river and bay. Local groups serve Maryland seafood and traditional picnic fare. The festival runs morning and afternoon both Saturday and Sunday.

Admission: free.
Location: Calvert Marine Museum.
Information: Calvert Marine Museum, (410) 326-2042.
Tourist Information: Calvert County Tourism, (410) 535-4583.

St. Mary's County Oyster Festival

Leonardtown, Md., third weekend in October.

During the St. Mary's County Oyster Festival, skilled oyster shuckers from 10 oyster-producing states compete in the U.S. National Oyster Shucking Championship. The fastest oyster shuckers from the St. Mary's competition go to Galway, Ireland, for the international championship, where they have never finished below third place. Shuckers come from oyster-packing houses and seafood restaurants; each must be sponsored by their employer or have won a local shucking contest.

The competition takes place during both afternoons of the festival. There are plenty of oysters—raw, fried, and scalded—and other treats like soft-crab sandwiches, fried chicken, oyster sandwiches, pork barbecue, and crab cakes. The food can be enjoyed with music performed by southern Maryland artists. There are also arts and crafts exhibits, including, of course, oyster-shell art.

Admission: $2.
Location: County Fair Grounds.
Directions: from Leonardtown follow Route 5 south for 2 miles.
Information: St. Mary's County Oyster Festival, (301) 863-5015.
Tourist Information: St. Mary's County Tourism, (301) 884-5555.

Tilghman Island Day

Tilghman, Md., next to last Saturday in October.

The Chesapeake Bay fishing village of Tilghman Island salutes its watermen on a Saturday in October. Through the day there are watermen competitions, such as the jigger throw, rowboat races, a boat-docking contest, a crab-picking contest, and an oyster-shucking contest. Tilghman is a major port for the Chesapeake Bay skipjacks, the last working sailboats in America, and Tilghman Island Day also features a skipjack race. Boatmen participate in a motorized workboat race that tests the speed and power of their crafts.

Local groups serve plenty of seafood, including crab cakes, oyster fritters, soft-crab sandwiches, oysters on the half shell, fried clams, and crab soup. Country bands play through the day; there are boat rides around the island; and watermen give demonstrations of their work. The festival begins midmorning and runs through the afternoon.

Admission: $4; families, $10.
Location: throughout Tilghman village.

Information: Tilghman Island Volunteer Fire Department, (410) 886-2677.
Tourist Information: Talbot County Tourism, (410) 822-4606.

Chesapeake Appreciation Days

Annapolis, Md., last weekend in October.

The skipjacks of the Chesapeake Bay are America's last working sailboats. Before World War I, some 1,500 skipjacks dredged for oysters on the bay; now there are fewer than 20. On the last weekend in October, just before oyster season, these last skipjacks race on a course between the Chesapeake Bay Bridge and Sandy Point Lighthouse. In recent years, the race has included ships launched between 1891 and 1956. Spectators watch from the beach at Sandy Point State Park.

Chesapeake Bay Appreciation Days includes other boat races and numerous land events. There are local entertainers, police K-9 demonstrations, and an air show. The festival has competitions in oyster shucking, workboat docking, and jousting, Maryland's state sport; there are also pig, duck, and goat races. The festival runs morning and afternoon Saturday and Sunday.

Admission: $5; children under 12, free.
Location: Sandy Point State Park.
Information: Maryland Watermen's Association, (410) 269-5570.
Tourist Information: Annapolis and Anne Arundel County Tourism Office, (410) 280-0445.

New Jersey

Victorian Week

Cape May, N.J., Friday of Columbus Day weekend to following weekend.

The resort town of Cape May is well known for its Victorian architecture, with homes and hotels sporting turrets, clapboards, and gingerbread woodwork. The town has carefully maintained its Victorian charm and celebrates that success during Victorian Week in October. Visitors can attend a gala where ladies wear long dresses with bustles and gentlemen dress up in starched collars and top hats, or go to Victorian murder mystery dinners at the Chalfonte Hotel. They can enjoy a Victorian vaudeville show or join in a boisterous, roof-raising Victorian sing-along.

Victorian Week lasts 10 days, with most activities on the two weekends. Among the many activities are tours of historic hotels and mansions, Victorian fashion shows, antiques and crafts shows, stained glass tours, Victorian theater performances, visits to the Cape May Point Lighthouse, and seminars on such things as Victorian stenciling and operating a country inn.

Admission: varies according to event.
Location: throughout the city.
Information: Mid-Atlantic Center for the Arts, (609) 884-5404.
Tourist Information: Chamber of Commerce of Greater Cape May, (609) 884-5508.

Chatsworth Cranberry Festival

Chatsworth, N.J., third weekend in October.

Chatsworth is the unofficial capital of the Pine Barrens, a vast forested area in southern New Jersey. Cranberry farming is a major industry there, and the town celebrates with two days of cranberry treats, contests, and authentic Pine Barren entertainment. Local groups serve cranberry ice, pie, bread, chutney, cheesecake, jam, and even cranberry barbecue. Prize winners from the Cranberry Recipe Contest are shown and offered for sale. A cranberry exhibit displays 20 different types of cranberries, plus the winners of the biggest and smallest cranberry contests.

Local musical groups have included the Third Rail, the Pine Coners, and the Pinelands Dulcimer Society. Piney tall tales and hunting stories are shared under the Storytelling Tree. The festival, which runs mornings and afternoons on Saturday and Sunday, also offers cranberry bog tours, arts and crafts, and historical exhibits.

Admission: parking, $3.
Location: Main Street.
Directions: Chatsworth is located at the junction of routes 563 and 532.
Information: Chatsworth Club II, (609) 859-9701.
Tourist Information: Burlington County Cultural and Heritage Commission, (609) 265-5068.

New York

Field, Forest and Stream Festival

Elizabethtown, N.Y., Saturday of Columbus Day weekend.

Field, Forest and Stream is a small festival celebrating Adirondack North Country folklife. Held at the Adirondack Center Museum, there are demonstrations of guideboat making, snowshoe construction, taxidermy, fly tying, food preservation, and Adirondack rustic furniture making. There usually is a game stew cook-off and a hunters' garb contest. Adirondack folk singers and string bands perform through the day, and members of the Adirondack Liars' Club spin tall tales.

Admission: adults, $2; children, $1.
Location: Adirondack Center Museum in downtown Elizabethtown.
Information: Essex County Historical Society, (518) 873-6466.
Tourist Information: Essex County Tourism, (800) 342-9561 or (518) 942-7794.

LaFayette Apple Festival

Cardiff, N.Y., Columbus Day weekend.

The organizers of the LaFayette Apple Festival strive to recreate the sights, sounds, and smells of an old-fashioned festival. The festival grounds sit amid the rolling hills of central New York at the village of Cardiff, site of the famous nineteenth-century hoax,

*Display of cranberry vari-
eties at New Jersey's Chatsworth Cranberry Festival.*

the Cardiff Giant. Apples from the nearby orchards are sold fresh
or prepared as pies, fritters, and dumplings. The LaFayette Op-
timists make steak sandwiches, the Masons serve hot sausage,
the Community Council bakes pizza, and a dozen other community groups cook up their own specialties. The festival's stage
features folk musicians, like hammered dulcimer players and
troubadours, through the weekend. More than 400 craftspeople
show and sell handcrafted furniture, nature photographs, jewelry, hand-made musical instruments, and a variety of other
work. The festival, which runs all day Saturday and Sunday,
attracts as many as 100,000 people.

Admission: adults, $1; children under 16, free.
Location: Festival Orchard Farm.
Directions: from Exit 15 off I-81 follow U.S. Route 20 west for 2
  miles.

Information: LaFayette Apple Festival, Inc., (315) 677-3300.
Tourist Information: Syracuse-Onondaga Convention and
Visitors Bureau, (800) 234-4797 or (315) 470-1800.

Oyster Festival
Oyster Bay, N.Y., weekend after Columbus Day.

A highlight of the Oyster Festival is an oyster-eating contest,
where contestants try to break festival and world records for
swallowing the most raw oysters in 2 minutes, 40 seconds. The
current festival record is 200 oysters. Visitors to the festival,
though, can enjoy smaller quantities of oysters—raw, fried, or in
chowder—at the various community food booths. Other local groups
(there are no commercial vendors) prepare clam chowder, gyros,
pasta, seafood gumbo, shrimp cocktail, steak sandwiches, and
other dishes.

The weekend event provides continuous entertainment on two
stages, and past performers have included Cliff Haslam singing
sea chanteys, the Long Island Mummers, the Pipes and Drums of
the Nassau County Police Department, the Robert Austin Magic
Show, the Mariachi Trio, and the Aloha Hawaiian Revue. Other
festival events include a juried arts and crafts show, a bicycle
race, and an oyster-shucking contest. The festival goes from morning until early evening Saturday and Sunday.

Admission: free.
Location: on streets of the business district.
Information: Oyster Festival, (516) 624-8082.
Tourist Information: Oyster Bay Chamber of Commerce, (516)
922-6464.

Pennsylvania

Pennsylvania Renaissance Faire
*Manheim, Pa., last weekend in June through second week-
end in October.*

See June—Pennsylvania.

Shawnee Autumn Balloon Festival
Shawnee-On-Delaware, Pa., weekend sometime in October.

The Shawnee Inn is one of the Pocono's old resorts. In October, just when the leaves are changing, the inn holds a colorful balloon festival, with balloon launches Friday, Saturday, and Sunday evenings and Saturday and Sunday mornings. Entertainment, carnival rides, balloon crew contests, festival food, arts and crafts, and children's activities are offered on the inn's grounds Saturday and Sunday afternoon. In the past, the festival has included skydiving demonstrations, boomerang demonstrations, pig racing, German oompah bands, and Civil War reenactments.

Admission: adults, $8; children ages 4–12, $3; under 4, free; group and senior discounts.
Location: Shawnee Inn.
Information: Shawnee Inn, (717) 421-1500, ext. 1724.
Tourist Information: Pocono Mountains Vacation Bureau, Inc., (800) 762-6667 or (717) 424-6050.

Springs Folk Festival
Springs, Pa., first Friday and Saturday in October.

Saw paintings, fungus paintings, grapevine wreaths, hex signs, wire art, and wheat weavings are some of the unusual crafts shown at the Springs Folk Festival. First held in 1957, the festival preserves and portrays the arts and crafts of pioneers and mountain folk. Skills such as maple sugaring, apple-butter boiling, log hewing, sauerkraut making, wool dyeing, and broom making are demonstrated on the festival's Forest Trail.

Entertainment scheduled through the morning and afternoon of both Friday and Saturday has included an a cappella Mennonite group, the Blue Mountain Cloggers, dulcimer players, and gospel groups. The Pennsylvania Dutch food usually includes sausage, Dutch fried potatoes, dried corn, and bean soup. At the outdoor oven, fresh baked bread is sold by the loaf or by the slice with apple butter.

Admission: adults, $4; children ages 6–12, $1; under 6, free; preregistered group rates.
Location: Springs Festival Grounds.
Directions: from Grantsville, Maryland, follow Route 669 north for 3 miles.
Information: Springs Folk Festival, (814) 662-4158.
Tourist Information: Laurel Highlands, Inc., (800) 333-5661 or (412) 238-5661.

Covered Bridge and Arts Festival

Elysburg, Pa., first weekend in October.

When the leaves begin turning in rural Columbia County, Elysburg puts on a festival celebrating the county's two dozen covered bridges, including the only twin bridges in the United States. At Knoebels Grove, community groups serve up corn and apple fritters, bean soup, pork and sauerkraut, buckwheat cakes and sausage, and barbecued chicken. Each afternoon the park's stage features square dancing, fife and drum corps, and country musicians. Each day, bus tours take visitors through the countryside on a tour of the covered bridges. The festival also includes children's entertainment, hayrides, a bicycle race, a fun auction, spinning and weaving demonstrations, and a Miss Covered Bridge Pageant on Saturday night.

Admission: free.
Location: Knoebels Grove Amusement Resort.
Information: Columbia/Montour Tourist Promotion Agency, (717) 784-8279.

National Apple Harvest Festival

Arendtsville, Pa., first two full weekends in October.

Adams County is Pennsylvania's most important apple-growing region, and for more than 25 years the county has celebrated the apple harvest with a fall festival. On each afternoon of the two weekends, entertainment is scheduled on four stages and includes bluegrass bands, folk dance groups, country-and-western singers, barbershop quartets, German oompah bands, folk musicians, and gospel choirs. Besides the usual festival food like chicken barbecue and sausage sandwiches, vendors sell special apple treats such as apple sauce, fried apples, candied apples, apple sausage, apple jellies, cider, apple fritters, apple pancakes with apple syrup, apple strudel, and even apple pizza.

The festival runs morning and afternoon on the Saturday and Sunday of both weekends. Among the craft demonstrators is a woman who makes dolls using carved apples as heads. Johnny Appleseed roams the festival grounds handing out seed packets, and he also supervises apple dunking and the apple-pie-eating contest in the Kid Country Building. The festival also offers steam engine rides, bus tours of the orchards, and an antique auto show.

Admission: $4; children ages 12 and under, free.

Location: South Mountain Fairgrounds.

Directions: from Gettysburg, follow U.S. Route 15 north for 10 miles to Heidlersburg, then follow Route 234 west for 10 miles.

Information: National Apple Harvest Festival, (717) 677-7820 or (717) 677-9413.

Tourist Information: Gettysburg Travel Council, (717) 334-6274.

Fort Ligonier Days

Ligonier, Pa., second weekend in October.

Fort Ligonier Days commemorate the unsuccessful French and Indian attack on the British forces at Fort Ligonier on October 12, 1758. A highlight of the weekend is the reenactment of the battle at the reconstructed fort, carried out by 75 authentically dressed and outfitted troops representing the Scottish Highlanders, Pennsylvania and Maryland Provincials, the French Marines and Army, and both English and French artillery units.

The festival runs Friday, Saturday, and Sunday, with activities all day. The community parade is Saturday morning, battle reenactments are presented Saturday and Sunday afternoons, and a lanternlight tour of the fort is held Saturday evening. Some 200 craftspeople display their work at several locations in town, and a special Colonial Market Place presents authentic eighteenth-century crafts and craftspeople in period clothing.

Outdoor entertainment through the weekend includes mandolin music, puppets, Irish folk music, ragtime piano, clogging, British Isles folk music, bagpipes and drums, bluegrass, hymn and gospel singing, and an old-fashioned band concert. Community groups sell a variety of food, and several churches offer sit-down dinners.

Admission: free.

Location: center of town.

Information: Ligonier Valley Chamber of Commerce, (412) 238-4200.

Tourist Information: Laurel Highlands, Inc., (800) 333-5661 or (412) 238-5661.

Super Sunday

Philadelphia, Pa., Sunday of Columbus Day weekend.

To most Americans, Super Sunday is the day in January when all gather in front of the tube for the big football game. But to Philadelphians, Super Sunday is the city's autumn festival, "the biggest block party in the world," when hundreds of thousands fill the Benjamin Franklin Parkway. Super Sunday kicks off with a Mummers Parade, a Philadelphia spectacle of colorfully costumed marchers playing stringed instruments. From then on it's an afternoon of good food and entertainment. Four stages strung out along the parkway offer military bands, blues singers, rock and roll groups, ragtime pianists, Dixieland bands, and Scottish bagpipers. At Sports Alley, wheelchair basketball teams demonstrate their skills, festivalgoers can try an urban surfing machine, and children can compete in the hula-hoop contest. The festival benefits the Academy of Natural Sciences, and the Academy's staff is on hand to show off boa constrictors and other creatures. Kids can even ride an elephant, camel, or pony.

Admission: free.

Location: Benjamin Franklin Parkway.
Information: Academy of Natural Sciences, (215) 665-1050.
Tourist Information: Philadelphia Convention and Visitors
   Bureau, (800) 321-9563 or (215) 636-1666.

Arts Festival/Octubafest

Carlisle, Pa., second or third Saturday in October.

Tuba players and brass ensembles play through an October afternoon at Carlisle's Octubafest. Past performers have included the
Hot House Traditional Jazz Band, the U.S. Navy Tuba Quartet,
and Bill Hicks Brass and Euphuba. The Arts Festival includes
150 crafts booths along High Street, and community groups serve
roast pork, hot sausage, funnel cakes, and other festival foods.
The day also offers a farmers' market, theatrical performances,
scarecrow making, and a Blessing of the Pets.
Admission: free.
Location: High Street in the center of town.
Information: Carlisle Economic Development Center, (717) 245-
   2648.
Tourist Information: Harrisburg-Hershey-Carlisle Tourism and
   Convention Bureau, (717) 232-1377.

Virginia

Fall Festival

Newport News, Va., first weekend in October.

The Fall Festival in Newport News celebrates American folk
artistry. Some 200 craftspeople attend the weekend event, dis-
playing their work and offering demonstrations in such things as
basket weaving, quilting, gunsmithing, and sheep shearing. Three
stages feature mostly folk music; past entertainers have included
Tom Chapin, the New Christy Minstrels, and the Brothers Four.
For the children, there are storytellers and a puppet theater. An

ethnic smorgasbord includes Greek, Chinese, and German food. The festival runs morning and afternoon of both Saturday and Sunday.

Admission: free; charge for parking.

Location: Newport News Park.

Directions: from Exit 60-B on I-64 turn left at the stoplight and follow Jefferson Avenue for 0.25 mile.

Information: Newport News Occasions, (804) 247-8451.

Tourist Information: Virginia Peninsula Tourism and Conference Bureau, (804) 873-0092.

Virginia Fall Foliage Festival

Waynesboro, Va., first and second weekends in October.

At about the time of the Virginia Fall Foliage Festival, the Blue Ridge above Waynesboro is ablaze with fall colors. Although the festival offers a variety of activities, just the sight of the colorful woodlands makes a trip to Waynesboro worthwhile. The town is at the end of both Skyline Drive, going north through the Shenandoah National Park, and the Blue Ridge Parkway, going south along the Blue Ridge of the Appalachians through Virginia and North Carolina. Both routes travel along the mountaintops, passing woodlands, meadows, lakes, and panoramic views of the Shenandoah Valley. There are scenic overlooks, picnic areas, campgrounds, and resorts along the way.

The Virginia Fall Foliage Festival is held on the first two weekends of October. One of the highlights of the festival is the outdoor Art Show, held the second weekend, with paintings, photography, sculpture, pottery, metalwork, glasswork, and other media. The festival also includes the British Car Club Show, special exhibits at the Shenandoah Valley Art Center, a Chili Cook-Off, a Gem and Mineral Show, a 10-kilometer run, and various concerts and open houses. The festival generally runs Friday, Saturday, and Sunday of the first weekend and Saturday and Sunday of the second weekend.

Admission: free; charges for some events.

Location: various locations in Waynesboro.

Information: Virginia Fall Foliage Festival, Inc., (703) 949-6505.
Tourist Information: Waynesboro-East Augusta Chamber of
Commerce, (703) 949-8203.

Richmond Children's Festival

Richmond, Va., second weekend in October.

Each year the Richmond Children's Festival highlights the art
and culture of a foreign country. One year it was Japan, and the
festival featured performances by the Taiko Dojo Drummers from
San Francisco, folk dancing of the O'Bon Dancers, and a Japanese
Cultural Center with Japanese games, a marketplace, and crafts.
Another year the country was Israel, with the Al-Anwar Druze
Folk Dancers, an Arts Kibbutz, and an Israeli Cultural Center.
The entertainment scheduled during the two days, though, is not
limited to the featured country. Five stages offer music, dancing,
storytelling, theater, clowns, jugglers, magic, and performances
by school groups. At various locations children can make puppets,
play games, or go for a hayride.

Admission: free.
Location: Byrd Park.
Directions: park at the University of Richmond Stadium and
take the shuttle bus.
Information: Arts Council of Richmond, (804) 643-4993.
Tourist Information: Metro Richmond Convention and Visitors
Bureau, (804) 782-2777.

Suffolk Peanut Fest

Suffolk, Va., second week in October.

At the Peanut Butter Sculpture Contest, Suffolk celebrities test
their skill at carving up hunks of peanut butter. Other typical
events include skydiving exhibitions, a dog show, pig races, a
peanut-cooking contest, an old-fashioned country fair, and a
children's fishing competition. Although events are scheduled

through the week, the festival itself runs at the Suffolk Municipal Airport Thursday through Sunday.

Entertainment is provided on three stages and has included Eddie Rabbitt, Juice Newton, and the Atlanta Rhythm Section. Past festivals have also included rodeo, lumberjack demonstrations, a demolition derby, and athletic events. Roasted peanuts and peanut dishes are served along with concession food. The Raritan club holds a Shrimp Feast during the week.

Admission: parking, $5.

Location: Suffolk Municipal Airport, routes 13 and 32, and other locations.

Information: Suffolk Festivals, Inc., (804) 539-6751.

Tourist Information: Suffolk Division—Hampton Roads Chamber of Commerce, (804) 539-2111.

Cravin' Catfish River Festival

Hopewell, Va., Saturday in late October.

Catfish gumbo soup, catfish on a stick, grilled catfish, fried battered catfish, catfish hush puppies, catfish-cake sandwiches, Cajun catfish, breaded catfish, and catfish nuggets are some of the dishes served at the Cravin' Catfish River Festival—not to mention an assortment of other seafood. The Saturday afternoon event is held on the Appomattox River and also offers continuous country music performances, river cruises, and children's activities.

Admission: free.

Location: Hopewell Yacht Club, Riverside Drive.

Information: Hopewell Visitors Center, (804) 541-2206.

West Virginia

Mountaineer Balloon Festival

Morgantown, W.Va., weekend in late September or October.

See September—West Virginia.

Mountain State Forest Festival

Elkins, W.Va., week of the first Thursday in October.

Since 1930, Elkins has been celebrating the beauty and natural resources of West Virginia with an October festival. The nine-day event includes the coronation of Queen Silvia by West Virginia's governor; two major parades; Grand Old Opry; three major dances; a downtown carnival; woodchopping, archery, horse pulling, and turkey-calling contests; the West Virginia Open State Championship Fiddle and Banjo Contest; motorcycle and ATV races; gospel sings; band concerts; and square dancing. Country cooking is available, including a chicken barbecue and a buckwheat cake and sausage feed.

Admission: free; charges for some events.
Location: various locations in Elkins.
Information: Mountain State Forest Festival Association, (304) 636-1824.
Tourist Information: Randolph County Convention and Visitors Bureau, (800) 422-3304 or (304) 636-2717.

Oglebayfest

Wheeling, W.Va., first full weekend in October.

Oglebay Park, a large estate given to the city of Wheeling by businessman Earl Oglebay, holds its annual Oglebayfest in early October. All kinds of music—big band, jazz, country, bluegrass—

are performed on several stages throughout the weekend. Performers have included the Short Crick Flatpickers, Suzuki Violinists, the Vince Villanova Big Band, and the hundred-voice Ohio Valley Chorale.

The festival runs through Saturday and Sunday, with most entertainment in the afternoon. Besides music, an old-fashioned country fair under a tent has cake judging, hog calling, a fiddle contest, and celebrity milking (with politicians and media personalities doing the honors). The Rathskeller at the park's Children Center features German food, music, and dancers. One of the largest draws is a judged artists' market, which opens half a day earlier. Over 60 artisans display and sell their work.

Admission: free.

Location: Oglebay Resort Park.

Directions: from the Oglebay exit on I-70 follow U.S. Route 40 for 0.5 mile, then go north on Route 88 for 2 miles.

Information: Oglebay Park, (304) 243-4032.

Tourist Information: Wheeling Convention and Visitors Bureau, (800) 828-3097 or (304) 233-7709.

West Virginia Pumpkin Festival

Milton, W.Va., first full weekend in October.

Nearly 5,000 schoolchildren decorate pumpkins for display during the West Virginia Pumpkin Festival. Kids also compete in the pumpkin-seed-spitting contest, while gardeners vie for the biggest pumpkin, and cooks enter their favorite pumpkin recipe. There even is an award for the craftsperson who best depicts the pumpkin in his or her work. There are all types of pumpkin pie and unusual foods like pumpkin butter, pumpkin fudge, and pumpkin barbecue.

The West Virginia Pumpkin Festival runs all day Friday, Saturday, and Sunday. Its juried arts and crafts show features Appalachian mountain work like hand-forged fireplace sets, bentwood furniture, hand-made brooms, and bobbin lace. There are demonstrations of weaving and spinning, blacksmithing, sorghum making, and apple- and pumpkin-butter making. Entertainers

Pumpkin Queen and prize-winning pumpkins at the West Virginia Pumpkin Festival.

perform on stage throughout the festival; past acts have included banjo player Elmer Bird, the Appalachian Fiddlers, and the Backyard Dixie Jazz Stompers. The festival also offers a Grand Parade Saturday morning, hot-air balloons, and a Pumpkin Queen Pageant.

Admission: adults, $3; senior citizens, $2; children ages 2–12, $1.
Location: Little League Complex.
Information: Milton City Hall, (304) 743-3032.

Tourist Information: Cabell-Huntington Convention and Visitors Bureau, (800) 635-6329 or (304) 525-7333.

Apple Butter Festival

Berkeley Springs, W.Va., Saturday and Sunday of Columbus Day weekend.

At the Berkeley Springs Apple Butter Festival, cooks put their big copper kettles on the fire at five o'clock in the morning and begin the day-long stirring of the apple butter. Apple butter and other local produce, like cider, honey, and fresh vegetables, are sold at the festival's farmers' market. Local groups also serve barbecued chicken, spit-roasted beef, Italian sausage, and other specialties.

While enjoying the good food, visitors can listen to bluegrass, Dixieland jazz, and country music performed by local groups at the park's bandstand or they can watch jugglers and fire-eaters perform in the streets. The festival runs all day Saturday and in the afternoon on Sunday. It includes a parade Saturday morning, a square dance Saturday evening, arts and crafts, and contests.

Admission: free.

Location: Berkeley Springs State Park.

Information: Berkeley Springs-Morgan County Chamber of Commerce, (800) 447-8797 or (304) 258-9147.

West Virginia Black Walnut Festival

Spencer, W.Va., second weekend in October.

Begun in 1955, the Black Walnut Festival celebrates Spencer's bountiful walnut harvest. The black walnut is more pungent than the common English walnut and can be used in cookies, cakes, and side dishes. One of the highlights of the festival is the delicious food made from the local black walnuts, including pancakes, fudge, brownies, and cakes. Plain hulled walnuts are sold, too.

Running Wednesday through Sunday, the festival offers musical performances most days, including country, "progressive-billy," rhythm and blues, Dixieland jazz, and fifties rock and roll. Other events include gospel sings, a carnival, a band and majorette competition, a Grand Parade, agricultural judging, arts and crafts, a black-powder shoot, athletic events, an antique auto show, and coronation of the Black Walnut Queen.

Admission: free.
Location: downtown, National Guard Armory, Arnoldsburg Road, Spencer High Athletic Field, and Roane County Country Club.
Information: West Virginia Black Walnut Festival, (304) 927-1780.
Tourist Information: Ripley Area Chamber of Commerce, (304) 372-3961.

Bridge Day
Fayetteville, W.Va., third Saturday in October.

Completed in 1977, the New River Gorge Bridge is the world's longest steel-arch bridge. It passes 876 feet above the New River, the second oldest river in the world. One Saturday in October the bridge is opened to walkers, who can enjoy the view of the gorge and the fall foliage. Over 250 BASE (building, antenna, span, and earth) jumpers parachute from the bridge to the river below, and some 300 men and women rappel off the bridge's edge. The festival also offers musical performances, dancers, jugglers, hayrides, and more than 250 vendors selling crafts, food, and souvenirs.

Admission: free.
Location: New River Gorge Bridge.
Directions: park in Fayetteville and ride Mountain Transit Authority buses to the bridge.
Information: Fayette County Chamber of Commerce, (304) 465-5617.
Tourist Information: Southern West Virginia Convention and Visitors Bureau, (800) 847-4898 or (304) 252-2244.

November

Maryland

Waterfowl Festival
Easton, Md., second full weekend in November.

When fall arrives on Maryland's Eastern Shore, the fields, marshes, and creeks near the town of Easton are filled with flocks of Canada geese, ducks, swans, and other migrating waterfowl. The town celebrates the fall migration in November with its Waterfowl Festival, the largest and best known in the country. Much of the festival revolves around wildlife art, and as many as 500 artisans from all over the world exhibit and sell paintings, carvings, duck stamps, and photography. Some of American's best wildlife artists attend.

The festival runs from Friday morning to Sunday evening. As well as artwork, there are retriever demonstrations, the World Championship Goose Calling Contest, the Mason-Dixon Regional Duck Calling Contest, and a decoy auction. Seafood, including Chesapeake crabs and oysters, is served.

Admission: 1 day, $8; 2 days, $14; 3 days, $18; children under 14, free with adult.
Location: buildings throughout the town of Easton.
Information: Waterfowl Festival, (410) 822-4567.
Tourist Information: Talbot County Tourism, (410) 822-4606.

New York

A Festival of Lights

Niagara Falls, N.Y., Saturday following Thanksgiving until early January.

Niagara Falls has long been known for the colored lights over the waterfalls themselves, but during the Christmas season the entire city lights up. Downtown trees, buildings, walkways, and indoor gardens are decorated with Christmas lighting and animated displays. All nine stories of the Occidental Chemical Center, for instance, are decorated and the lights are synchronized to music. At the seven-story Wintergarden, lights and decorations are placed among the tropical plants and trees.

The lights continue for a month and a half. During that time the city hosts daily entertainment, including special concerts that have featured Roy Clark, Tammy Wynette, John Denver, and Tennessee Ernie Ford. Other events include art shows, hockey tournaments, guided walking tours, Santa's Magical Midway, ballet performances, and a live Nativity.

Admission: free.
Location: various locations in downtown Niagara Falls.
Information: Niagara Falls Area Chamber of Commerce, (716) 285-8484.

Virginia

Urbanna Oyster Festival

Urbanna, Va., first Friday and Saturday in November.

Tall ships like the *Alexandria* come to the waterfront of Urbanna at the foot of Virginia Street for the town's annual oyster festival. Held in early November at the beginning of the oyster season, the festival features numerous community groups and vendors selling oysters raw, fried, or in chowder, as well as other seafood and

Oyster shucking at the Urbanna Oyster Festival.

festival food. On three stages, local groups perform rhythm and blues, country and western, and sixties rock. The festival parade through the village's main street on Saturday morning includes the Oyster Festival Queen, Little Miss Spat, community floats, and local high school bands.

Admission: free.

Location: throughout the village.

Information: Middlesex Chamber of Commerce, (804) 758-5540.

December

Maryland

First Night Annapolis

Annapolis, Md., New Year's Eve.

The first First Night was held in Boston in 1976. A group of performing artists were disappointed at not finding work for New Year's Eve, so they created their own event: a nonalcoholic, family-oriented festival of the performing arts. They performed in churches, community halls, and outdoors in the downtown area. New Year's Eve merrymakers walked from one location to the next, selecting the performances they wanted to attend from a printed schedule. The success of Boston's First Night has continued every year since 1976, now attracting over 500,000 First Nighters. The event has spread across the United States and Canada to over 50 cities.

Although Annapolis is the capital of Maryland, it is a small, quiet colonial town. On New Year's Eve, entertainment celebrating the coming new year fills the State House Rotunda, old churches, the courthouse, historic homes, and community buildings. First Night revelers walk the cold, dark streets from one warm location to the next, enjoying storytelling, bossa nova, medieval music, bluegrass, historic lectures, drama, folk music, traditional dancing, mime, gospel music, and ice skating performances. At midnight the crowd gathers at the City Dock for the ringing of church bells, a fireworks display, and a bagpipe band playing "Auld Lang Syne."

Admission: $8; children ages 6 and under, free.

Location: various locations in Annapolis's historic district.
Information: First Night Annapolis, (410) 268-8553.
Tourist Information: Annapolis and Anne Arundel County
Tourism Office, (410) 280-0445.

New York

A Festival of Lights

*Niagara Falls, N.Y., Saturday following Thanksgiving until
early January.*

See November—New York.

First Night Albany

Albany, N.Y., New Year's Eve.

Albany's First Night begins at six o'clock in the evening with a
parade through the city's streets. Then, at more than 50 locations
downtown, a variety of entertainment continues through the rest
of the evening. Music includes rock, classical, jazz, gospel, rhythm
and blues, and country. First Nighters can join square dances,
Irish jigs, polkas, or a Viennese waltz ball at the old train station.
Special children's entertainment features a circus, puppet shows,
magic, and storytellers. The evening also offers comedy, psychic
demonstrations, and one-act plays. First Night ends at midnight
with a fireworks display over the Hudson.

Admission: $10; in advance, $8; children ages 5 and under, free.
Location: numerous locations in downtown Albany.
Information: Mayor's Office of Special Events, (518) 434-2032.
Tourist Information: Albany County Convention and Visitors
Bureau, (800) 258-3582 or (518) 434-1217.

Storyteller at the Annapolis, Maryland, First Night.

Pennsylvania

Christkindl Market

Mifflinburg, Pa., Thursday through Saturday of week after Thanksgiving Day.

The Christkindmarkt is a German Christmas celebration, a tradition that began in Munich over six centuries ago. It is a Christmas market, usually held on a town's market square in the evenings under the glow of glittering lights and Christmas ornaments. Huts covered with fir boughs and white lights showcase the town's specialties, including Christmas decorations, local crafts, and food. Nearby churches offer warmth and music. Most Christkindmarkts last a weekend, although in larger cities they may run from Advent until Christmas.

Mifflinburg, whose citizens are of German extraction, holds its Christkindl Market on Market Street, near two of the town's old churches. One churchyard holds a 21-foot-tall German pyramid, styled after the traditional table ornament that uses the heat of candles to spin a carousel of Christmas figures. Mifflinburg's pyramid features the march of the three Holy Kings, the Nativity scene, and the shepherds and their flocks, each on one of the pyramid's three levels.

Huts decorated with boughs offer table-sized pyramids, handmade ornaments, and gift items like glassware, jewelry, and hand-knit sweaters. A English madrigal dinner is held Thursday night, and community groups sell sandwiches, Christmas cookies, and hot mulled cider at the market. Performances on the market stage and in the churches feature Christmas music by brass ensembles and local choruses. Santa arrives by horse-drawn sleigh on Friday evening and meets with children through the evening and on Saturday afternoon. The market is open Thursday and Friday evening and in the morning and afternoon on Saturday.

Admission: free.

Location: Market Street.

Information: Mifflinburg Heritage and Revitalization Association, (717) 966-1666.

Tourist Information: Susquehanna Valley Visitors Bureau, (800) 458-4748.

Virginia

Hampton Holly Days

Hampton, Va., usually first weekend in December.

Hampton Holly Days begins on Friday evening, when Santa and Mrs. Claus arrive on the *Miss Hampton* in the company of a flotilla of decorated boats strung with Christmas lights. Hampton's waterfront is filled with merrymakers singing carols or enjoying performances by organists, hand-bell choirs, jazz musicians, choruses, theater groups, mimes, and magicians. The festival continues through the rest of the weekend with a Saturday morning breakfast with Santa, a Saturday afternoon children's program, and concerts and dances at various locations. Hampton Holly Days is held on the same weekend as the popular Grand Illumination at nearby Williamsburg.

Admission: free.
Location: waterfront area.
Information: Hampton Frolics, Inc., (804) 727-6429.
Tourist Information: Hampton Visitors Center, (804) 727-1102.

First Night Leesburg

Leesburg, Va., New Year's Eve.

The quaint, historic town of Leesburg, Virginia, welcomes the New Year with an evening of dance, music, and children's entertainment. As with all First Night celebrations, this festival is nonalcoholic and family-oriented, with performances scheduled through New Year's Eve at churches, the town council chambers, and the courthouse. Past performers have included rock-and-roll bands, blues guitarists, jugglers, magicians, choruses, comedians, storytellers, and bluegrass bands. The evening concludes with a candlelight procession to the Courthouse Green, where the New Year is rung in with sing-alongs and serenades.

Admission: $4; children under 6, free.
Location: historic district.
Information: First Night Leesburg, Inc., (703) 777-6795.
Tourist Information: Loudoun County Tourist Information Center, (800) 752-6118 or (703) 777-0519.

First Night Virginia

Charlottesville, Va., New Year's Eve.

First Night Virginia is held in Charlottesville, once home of Thomas Jefferson. Without a doubt, Jefferson would approve of the community event, its volunteer workers, and its use of local musicians, singers, dancers, storytellers, magicians, poets, and actors. First Night Virginia has featured a Russian Balalaika band, a carillon performance, Appalachian storytellers, morris dancers, cloggers, karate teams, swing orchestras, bluegrass bands, classic rock performers, blues singers, and gospel choirs. First Night Virginia begins with a parade in early evening and ends with fireworks at midnight.

Admission: $5.

Location: various locations downtown.

Information: First Night Virginia, (804) 296-8269.

Tourist Information: Charlottesville-Albemarle Convention and Visitors Bureau, (804) 293-6789.

TOPICAL INDEX

Arts and Crafts

Ballooning

Children

Community

Hometown Holidays, Rockville, Md. (May)   25
Ithaca Festival, Ithaca, N.Y. (June)   51
The Main Event, Rochester, N.Y. (July)   91
Mason-Dixon Festival, Morgantown, W.Va. (Sept.)   179
Mt. Pleasant Glass Festival, Mt. Pleasant, Pa. (Sept.)   167
Punxsutawney Groundhog Festival, Punxsutawney, Pa. (June)   63
Rain Day Festival, Waynesburg, Pa. (July)   103
Roanoke's Festival in the Park, Roanoke, Va. (May)   37
Three Rivers Coal Festival, Fairmont, W.Va. (May)   39
Towsontown Spring Festival, Towson, Md. (May)   21
Victorian Week, Cape May, N.J. (Oct.)   188
Virginia Highlands Festival, Abingdon, Va. (July)   108
We Love Erie Days, Erie, Pa. (August)   127

Ethnic

American Indian Inter-Tribal Cultural Organization Powwow,
    McHenry, Md. (July)   74
Bavarian Fun Fest, Sharon, Pa. (July)   102
British and Irish Festival, Norfolk, Va. (April)   18
Feast of Our Lady of Mt. Carmel and St. Paulinus of Nola, New York,
    N.Y. (July)   83
Feast of St. Anthony, New York, N.Y. (June)   53
Feast of San Gennaro, New York, N.Y. (Sept.)   153
Festival of Nations, Norfolk, Va. (July)   104
French Festival, Cape Vincent, N.Y. (July)   86
German Alps Festival, Hunter, N.Y. (July)   84
German Festival, Baltimore, Md. (August)   114
Gore Mountain Region Oktoberfest, North Creek, N.Y. (Sept.)   158
Greek Festival, Wilmington, Del. (June)   42
Hagley's Irish Workers' Festival, Wilmington, Del. (April)   13
Heritage Days Festival, Trenton, N.J. (June)   48
Hungarian Festival of New Brunswick, New Brunswick, N.J.
    (June)   47
International Celtic Festival, Hunter, N.Y. (August)   120
Irish Festival, Baltimore, Md. (Sept.)   145
Italian Festival, Baltimore, Md. (July)   75
Italian Festival, Hunter, N.Y. (June)   57
La Festa Italiana, Scranton, Pa. (June)   159
Latin American Festival, Washington, D.C. (July)   77
Lower East Side Jewish Festival, New York, N.Y. (June)   50
Nanticoke Indian Powwow, Millsboro, Del. (Sept.)   140
National Polka Festival, Hunter, N.Y. (August)   117
New Jersey Ethnic Festival, Jersey City, N.J. (Sept.)   149
Oktoberfest, Newark, Del. (Setpember)   141
Oktoberfest, Upper Marlboro, Md. (Sept.)   147
Pittsburgh Folk Festival, Pittsburgh, Pa. (May)   34
Polish-American Festival, Doylestown, Pa. (Sept.)   160

Flowers

Folklife

Food. *Also see* Seafood

Chester County Restaurant Festival, West Chester, Pa. (Sept.)   164
Corn Festival, Shippensburg, Pa. (August)   131
Cravin' Catfish River Festival, Hopewell, Va. (Oct.)   200
Delmarva Chicken Festival, 1992: Salisbury, Md., 1993: Cambridge, Md. (June)   44
Feast of the Ramson, Richwood, W.Va. (April)   18
Festival of Grapes, Silver Creek, N.Y. (Sept.)   155
Highland Maple Festival, Monterey, Va. (March)   12
Ice Cream Festival, Wilmington, Del. (July)   73
International Food Festival, Richmond, Va. (Sept.)   173
LaFayette Apple Festival, Cardiff, N.Y. (Oct.)   190
Lebanon Bologna Fest, Lebanon, Pa. (August)   124
Leitersburg Peach Festival, Leitersburg, Md. (August)   113
Maryland State Chili Championship and Crafts Show, Cumberland, Md. (August)   115
McClure Bean Soup Festival, McClure, Pa. (Sept.)   163
Naples Grape Festival, Naples, N.Y. (Sept.)   156
National Apple Harvest Festival, Arendtsville, Pa. (Oct.)   194
Ninth Avenue International Food Festival, New York, N.Y. (May)   27
Owego Strawberry Festival, Owego, N.Y. (June)   57
Pennsylvania Maple Festival, Meyersdale, Pa. (March or April)   11
Phelps Sauerkraut Festival, Phelps, N.Y. (August)   118
Pork, Peanut, and Pine Festival, Surry, Va. (July)   105
Preston County Buckwheat Festival, Kingwood, W.Va. (Sept.)   181
Red, White, and Blueberry Festival, Hammonton, N.J. (July)   79
Robert Gibbon Johnson Day Tomato Festival, Salem, N.J. (Sept.)   150
Shad Festival, Lambertville, N.J. (April)   15
Spiedie Fest and Balloon Rally, Binghamton, N.Y. (August)   118
Suffolk Peanut Fest, Suffolk, Va. (Oct.)   199
Taste of Buffalo, Buffalo, N.Y. (July)   88
West Virginia Black Walnut Festival, Spencer, W.Va. (Oct.)   204
West Virginia Pumpkin Festival, Milton, W.Va. (Oct.)   202
West Virginia Strawberry Festival, Buckhannon, W.Va. (May)   41
Whitesbog Blueberry Festival, Browns Mills, N.J. (July)   79
Whitetop Mountain Ramp Festival, Whitetop, Va. (May)   37

Historic
August Court Days, Leesburg, Va. (August)   135
Can-Am Festival, Sackets Harbor, N.Y. (July)   89
Chestertown Tea Party Festival, Chestertown, Md. (May)   24
Court Days, Woodstock, Va. (June)   70
Fort Ligonier Days, Ligonier, Pa. (Oct.)   195
Maryland Days Weekend, St. Mary's City, Md. (March)   9
Mifflinburg Buggy Days, Mifflinburg, Pa. (May)   32
National Pike Festival, Washington, Allegany, Garrett Counties, Md. (May)   23
National Pike Festival, Somerset, Fayette, Washington Counties, Pa. (May)   31

Urban Neighborhood

Adams Morgan Day, Washington, D.C. (Sept.)   142
Atlantic Antic Giant Festival, Brooklyn, N.Y. (Sept.)   157
Fabulous Fifth Avenue Street Fair, Brooklyn, N.Y. (May)   28
Fell's Point Fun Festival, Baltimore, Md. (Oct.)   182
Harlem Week, New York, N.Y. (August)   119
Philadelphia Freedom Festival, Philadelphia, Pa. (July)   97
Stuyvesant Park Festival, New York, N.Y. (April)   16
Super Sunday, Philadelphia, Pa. (Oct.)   196
Welcome Back to Brooklyn, Brooklyn, N.Y. (June)   54

Wine

Festival of Grapes, Silver Creek, N.Y. (Sept.)   155
Garden State Winegrowers Fall Festival, alternating locations in N.J. (Sept.)   151
Garden State Winegrowers Spring Festival, alternating locations in N.J. (June)   49
Maryland Wine Festival, Westminster, Md. (Sept.)   146
Naples Grape Festival, Naples, N.Y. (Sept.)   156
Vintage Virginia, Front Royal, Va. (June)   65
Virginia Wine Festival, Middleburg, Va. (August)   137
Wine Country Harvest Festival, North East, Pa. (Sept.)   168

Winter

Cooperstown Winter Carnival, Cooperstown, N.Y. (Feb.)   8
Saranac Lake Winter Carnival, Saranac Lake, N.Y. (Feb.)   6
Snowtown U.S.A., Watertown, N.Y. (Jan. to Feb.)   4
Winterfest, Syracuse, N.Y. (Jan. to Feb.)   5

FESTIVAL INDEX

Books from The Countryman Press and Backcountry Publications

Explorer's Guides

Explorer's Guides focus on independently owned inns, motels, and restaurants, and on family and cultural activities reflecting the character and unique qualities of the area.

The Hudson River and Catskill Mountains:
  An Explorer's Guide $15.00
Maine: An Explorer's Guide, Sixth Edition $17.00
New Hampshire: An Explorer's Guide $17.00
Vermont: An Explorer's Guide, Fifth Edition $16.95

Walks & Rambles Series

Walks & Rambles in Dutchess and Putnam Counties $11.00
Walks & Rambles in Rhode Island, Second Edition $11.00
More Walks & Rambles in Rhode Island $11.00
Walks & Rambles in Westchester & Fairfield Counties,
  Second Edition $11.00
Walks & Rambles in the Upper Connecticut River Valley $10.00
Walks & Rambles on Cape Cod and the Islands $11.00
Walks & Rambles on the Delmarva Peninsula $11.00

Other Guides

Family Resorts of the Northeast $12.95
Mount Washington, by Peter E. Randall $9.95
New England's Special Places $13.00
New Jersey's Special Places $13.00
Newport, Rhode Island $11.95
Ponds & Lakes of the White Mountains $16.00
Waterfalls of the White Mountains $15.00
The Wines and Wineries of the Hudson River Valley $14.95

Our titles are available in bookshops and in many sporting goods stores, or they may be ordered directly from the publisher. Shipping and handling costs are $2.50 for 1-2 books, $3 for 3-6 books, and $3.50 for 7 or more books. To order, or for a complete catalog, please write to The Countryman Press, Inc., P.O. Box 175, Dept. APC, Woodstock, VT 05091, or call our toll-free number, (800) 245-4151. Prices and availability are subject to change.